MISSTATING
THE STATE OF THE UNION

BY MEDIAMATTERS.ORG

MEDIA MATTERS ACTION NETWORK

WITH AN INTRODUCTION BY
DAVID BROCK

Akashic Books
New York

Published by Akashic Books
©2004 Media Matters Action Network

ISBN: 1-888451-80-7
Library of Congress Control Number: 2004112182
Printed in Canada
First Printing

Akashic Books
PO Box 1456
New York, NY 10009
Akashic7@aol.com
www.akashicbooks.com

TABLE OF CONTENTS

Introduction by David Brock   9

NO JOBS? NO PROBLEM!   15
Conservative Commentators'
Rose-Colored View of the Bush Economy

FISCALLY *WHAT?*   33
Spendthrift Conservatives and Their Apologists in the Press

SQUANDERED UNITY   48
Right-Wing Pundits' Blind Support
for Bush's National Security Policy

BAD MEDICINE   65
How Right-Wing Pundits Can Really Make You Sick

MISEDUCATION   84
The Conservative Media's Smoke Screen
Around Right-Wing Attacks on Public Schools

ENVIRONMENTAL POLICY   97
Conservative Commentators Treat Science As Optional

"39 MILLION GREEDY GEEZERS"   108
What the Right-Wing Media Really Thinks of America's Seniors

NOT WHAT YOU HEAR ON TV   120
The Comparative Record on Crime and Public Safety

NO SENSE OF SHAME   132
Conservative Pundits' Destructive Rhetoric About Values

Acknowledgments   149
Endnotes   150

INTRODUCTION

On FOX News, the economy is "growing like crazy."

On the editorial page of the *Wall Street Journal*, new jobs at great wages are being created at a blistering pace.

On *The Rush Limbaugh Show*, seniors have no difficulty getting the medicine they need.

Back on FOX News, parents needn't worry about the arsenic and mercury in their kids' drinking water.

In the rest of America, of course, none of these things are true. Yet conservative pundits, commentators, and "journalists" tell these lies and others on a daily basis, misleading and misinforming the American people.

For years, these right-wing propagandists have been peddling their "up-is-down," "black-is-white" take on the state of the union.

They've been lying to you at every turn: lying about the economy, lying about the budget, about health care, about education, the environment, national security . . . lying about everything, and skewing the debate over important issues in the process.

We're here to set the record straight.

In the following pages, we'll look at the misinformation being peddled by right-wing pundits like Sean Hannity, Rush Limbaugh, Bill O'Reilly, Ann Coulter, and Brit Hume (and some mainstream news sources, too).

We'll cut through their spin, lies, and distortions to bring you the truth about the issues that matter most.

Hannity, Limbaugh, Coulter and the rest relentlessly mislead their audiences, pushing an ultra-right agenda with no regard for truth—or for the disastrous effect the policies they advocate have on America.

On issue after issue, progressive policies have proven far more successful than conservative policies. Progressive policies have led to the largest budget surplus in history, declining crime rates, improved education, increased funding to fight deadly diseases, an effective retirement security program for seniors, and responsible environmental protections.

Conservative policies, meanwhile, have led to soaring deficits, a stagnant job market, arsenic in our drinking water, increased crime, and a diminished world stature for our nation. They've made America less secure at home and less respected abroad.

And there's something else, something even worse than right-wing pundits' relentless support of failed policies, going on here, too.

Because they are too often used without full consideration of their meaning, the words "demagoguery" and "sophistry" have lost their impact. But demagoguery and sophistry are exactly what the right-wing pundits are up to.

Conservative commentators, faced with the failure of the policies they espouse, have not chosen to move forward to explore new solutions to our shared problems. Instead, they have chosen to employ debating tactics more appropriate to nursery school than to national discourse. They ignore the facts, they yell, they call their opponents names, they claim not to have said words they uttered only moments before, and they continue to insist, no matter what, that they are right.

They overstep the bounds of decency. Ann Coulter sneers that America's seniors are "39 million greedy geezers." Bill

O'Reilly calls the poor "irresponsible and lazy." Rush Limbaugh smears environmentalists as "wackos." O'Reilly has called the Pope a "Saddam enabler." Michael Savage tells his listeners, "When you hear 'human rights,' think only someone who wants to molest your son, and send you to jail if you defend him. Write that down, make a note of it."

Their statements are often prefaced by phrases like "we all know," and end with "write this down," or "and you know it." They lie, and then just assume you agree.

They lie, and they defend their right to lie by saying they are "pundits" or "commentators" or "entertainers" or just offering their "opinion." Well, they have a right to their opinion, as everyone does.

But when Rush Limbaugh claims the federal government spends three times as much on education as on defense, that isn't a matter of "opinion." That's a lie. A flat-out lie. When pundit after pundit says the budget went into deficit because of the terrorist attacks of September 11, 2001, that's not a matter of "opinion." It's a lie: The Congressional Budget Office announced in *August* 2001 that the budget had gone into deficit.

But the right-wing commentators and pundits keep right on lying, and when, every once in a while, they admit that they don't have the truth on their side, they claim they're just giving their "opinion," and opinions can't be wrong. But not *everything* is an opinion. That way lies madness.

No, they must know that there are such things as facts. They just don't care.

They must believe that Americans are fools; that we are incapable of seeing the truth and will believe their lies if only they repeat them often and loudly enough. They must believe that yelling, name-calling, and lying are more persuasive than logic and reason and fact and civility.

Either way, they are wrong, and they should be ashamed of themselves.

But they are not ashamed. They keep yelling, and name-calling, and lying. And they will keep doing so until America stops falling for it.

Unfortunately, their form of discourse has become the dominant form. The airwaves are filled with shouts and shouted responses; with hosts screaming at guests, guests yelling back at hosts, and no room for the truth in between. The media, by and large, has abdicated its role as truth seeker and its position as impartial judge of fact and fiction.

Vice President Cheney can say publicly, "John Kerry is, by *National Journal* ratings, the most liberal member of the United States Senate . . . And it's not based on one vote, or one year, it's based on 20 years of service in the United States Senate"—a charge that is flatly, demonstrably false; it's a lie—and know that nary a soul in the press corps will challenge him on his statements.

What's more, many of them will repeat his charge as fact; others (even those who must know the truth: Kerry isn't even in the top *ten* in the *National Journal* rankings, much less number one) will simply quote Cheney's attack, without bothering to provide the facts.

When the media won't do their job, when many of them actively and intentionally lie and mislead, it's time to look elsewhere for the facts.

That's where both this book and the work *Media Matters for America* does every day come in.

The American public is confronted at every turn by misleading, inaccurate, and sometimes just plain false information about issues that have tremendous impact on their lives. This misinformation, spread by conservative pundits, commentators, columnists, and broadcasters, skews the public debate and makes it extraordinarily difficult for even the most civic-minded citizens to reach well-informed opinions about our nation's priorities. With this book, we provide a counterbalance to the hot air, facts to rebut the lies, and truth to counter the misleading statements. With this book, we expose the misinformation flooding our airwaves, and the conservative media figures who delight in spreading it.

But this book is only a small part of the process.

Media Matters for America is a web-based, not-for-profit progressive research and information center dedicated to comprehensively monitoring, analyzing, and correcting conservative misinformation in the U.S. media—news or commentary presented in the media that is not accurate, reliable, or credible, and that forwards the conservative agenda.

Media Matters for America's website—www.mediamatters.org—is the principal vehicle for disseminating research and information through a range of initiatives, from daily monitoring and analysis to activism programs that can help you hold the media accountable.

This book is but a small hint of what the talented and dedicated people at *Media Matters for America* produce every day. Our staff works tirelessly to collect, analyze, or correct conservative misinformation wherever we find it—and to publicize our work in an effort to bring about real change. We hope you'll join the more than one million people who visited our website in our first three months, and that you will help us correct the right-wing spin and distortion in the media.

David Brock
Washington, D.C.
August 2004

NO JOBS? NO PROBLEM!
Conservative Commentators' Rose-Colored View of the Bush Economy

> *"The best thing President Bush can do for the economy is to ignore Democratic cries to fix it."*
> —Conservative columnist Linda Chavez[1]

Right-wing pundits peddle two myths about the U.S. economy. The first is that the economy is just fine; in fact, they claim, it's in a gravity-busting recovery. The second is that those somehow left out of the amazing recovery shouldn't fault President Bush because this recession started under his predecessor, Bill Clinton.

These two claims fuel the 2004 conservative spin machine and have flooded the news media, appearing constantly in newspapers, on television, and across the Internet. The only problem with the claims is that—regardless of how often conservatives repeat them—they are simply lies.

IGNORING JOBLESS AMERICANS, CONSERVATIVE PUNDITS THINK THE ECONOMY IS FINE

Columnist George Will (who, though it is not germane to his view of the economy, used a briefing book stolen from Jimmy Carter to coach Ronald Reagan for a crucial debate against

Jimmy Carter in 1980[2], then praised Reagan's performance without disclosing his involvement, making very clear where he fits on the progressive/conservative continuum, as well as speaking volumes about his integrity) expresses the opinion that all is well with the economy and that Americans are stupid if they don't recognize the prosperity under their noses.

"The economy has been growing for two years," Will asserted earlier this year, even though he admitted that "a plurality of Americans say the economy is getting worse." Will, taking a stance typical of conservative elites, suggested that this disconnect between his opinion of the economy and that of the majority of Americans does not mean that he is wrong, but that they are stupid: "Every presidential campaign is an epidemic of economic illiteracy," Will sniffed.[3]

The conservative editorial writers at the *Wall Street Journal* likewise dispute any notion that the 2004 economy is sluggish, jobless, or recession-prone. In June 2004 they opined: "Consider that over the last six months, some 665,000 new jobs . . . were created in the higher paying service industries." The Bush administration "should be happy to engage in this debate," they editorialized, "since it's one that it can win on the merits."[4]

Conservative talk show host Sean Hannity also sees obvious merits in the Bush economy: "We now have the longest quarter of growth in 20 years."[5] (Hannity's astute economic analysis failed to explain how the three-month quarter in question miraculously lasted longer than any other standard three-month quarter.)

Then there's Ann Coulter, who has raised right-wing callousness to an art form. Last year she coldly advocated the idea that a few million Americans without jobs aren't reason for concern:

> To imply that a 6.1 percent unemployment rate is catastrophic is pure propaganda . . . This is the same type of media hype that puts entire cities in panic because the weatherman keeps repeat-

ing that a "ferocious" winter storm could "dump" up to 6 inches of snow on the northeast in the middle of January. When, in fact, 6 inches of snow in January and a 6 percent unemployment rate are both just a sleepy "normal."[6]

Of course, it's easy for Coulter to be indifferent to the inability of six percent of the workforce to find a job; as long as right-wing sugar daddies like Rupert Murdoch, the Reverend Moon, and Richard Mellon Scaife are around, Coulter needn't worry about where her next paycheck will come from. But if you think Coulter is unique in her icy indifference, think again. In response to complaints that the U.S. has lost good-paying manufacturing jobs, George Will's stance seems to be that the destruction of jobs is no cause for concern: "Manufacturing employment as a percentage of total employment is declining. True. Has been for 60 years. We make steel today. We make [sic] steel 20 years ago. We just make a third more steel today with two-thirds fewer steelworkers who have gone on to other points of employment . . . That's a triumph of American productivity. Not a problem."[7]

Will's statement illustrates a crucial difference between liberals and conservatives. Conservatives look at economic statistics and the stock market and declare the economy healthy. Liberals look at the same statistics and wonder why, when economic fundamentals are good, there are still so many Americans without jobs and why those working Americans are struggling to get by.

Liberals and conservatives agree that American capitalism has created more wealth, security, and well-being than any other in history. The difference between them is that conservatives, content with their own comfort, think we've already completed the capitalist experiment. Liberals think we can continue to do better, so that economic prosperity brings the same benefits to both Wall Street and Main Street.

WHEN THINGS ARE BAD, RIGHT-WING PUNDITS BLAME PRESIDENT CLINTON

"President Bush inherited a recession."
—Too many conservative pundits to count

According to the National Bureau of Economic Research (widely acknowledged as the definitive authority on when recessions begin and end), the first U.S. recession of the 21st century officially began in March 2001—two months *after* Bill Clinton left the presidency.[8]

Sean Hannity—whose radio show reaches almost 12 million listeners—brags that he "always lands on the 'right side' of the issues."[9] That may be, but unfortunately, Hannity is rarely on the *correct* side. The cohost of FOX News Channel's *Hannity and Colmes* is a Johnny One-Note when it comes to blaming Bill Clinton for the current problems of the Bush economy, starting with his frequent attempts to blame Bill Clinton for the 2001 recession.

In the past two years, Hannity has repeatedly claimed that President Bush "inherited" a recession from former President Clinton. A partial list of examples:

- *"The president inherited a recession."*
—Sean Hannity, April 6, 2004[10]

- *"The president inherited a recession."*
—Sean Hannity, March 26, 2004[11]

- *"So this is where I view the economic scenario as we head into this election. The president inherited a recession."*
—Sean Hannity, March 16, 2004[12]

- *"The president inherited a recession. That's now on record."*
—Sean Hannity, March 3, 2004[13]

- *"The president inherited a recession."*
—Sean Hannity, February 23, 2004[14]

- *"First of all, this president—you know and I know and everybody knows—inherited a recession."*
—Sean Hannity, November 6, 2002[15]

Not to be left out, the *Wall Street Journal* editorial page has jumped on the bandwagon of the so-called Clinton Recession, asserting: "The 'Bush recession' began for all practical purposes on Mr. Clinton's watch."[16]

Though they position themselves as "independent voices," Hannity and the *Journal's* editorial team are reading from the same talking points as the Bush-Cheney re-election team. Last summer, President Bush kicked off his re-election by reviving what the *Washington Post* called "his pastime of blaming his predecessor, Bill Clinton," for the economic recession. At a Miami reception, the president proclaimed, "Two-and-a-half years ago, we inherited an economy in recession."[17]

Problem is, Hannity, the *Journal*, and Bush are wrong when they say that the recession of 2001 began on President Clinton's watch. And so are George Will, Ann Coulter, and their right-wing friends when they allege that the U.S. economy is not a cause for concern.

DESPITE WHAT PUNDITS SAY, IT WAS BUSH'S RECESSION

At times, President Bush has acknowledged that the recession began on his watch, noting in a December 2001 radio address: "This week, the official announcement came that our economy has been in recession since March [2001]."[18]

But the following year, Bush instructed Republican governors: "I want you all to remember that when Dick Cheney and I got sworn in, the country was in a recession."[19]

In a burst of revisionist economic history, in May of 2003 the president pinpointed the exact date on which his inherited recession began: "Our nation went into a recession, starting January 1 of 2001."[20] If you're counting, that was (conveniently) 19 days before George W. Bush took office—and *two months* before the recession actually began.

Conservative pundits continue to press Bush's inaccurate point. In December 2002, a full year after the NBER identified the start of the recession as March 2001, Peter Huessy wrote in the *Washington Times*:

> Without the tax reductions enacted by President Bush in the spring of 2001, the U.S. economy would have remained in recession, an economic downturn given to us by President Clinton and his Democratic friends in Congress like Mr. Kerry, who obviously found it more politically exciting to try and destroy Microsoft, chase interns around the White House, ignore terrorism, dismantle the defenses of our country, and leave an incoming president with a growing deficit, slowed economy, a shaky security situation worldwide and a slumped stock market.[21]

As recently as August 1, former Speaker of the House (and current FOX News Channel analyst) Newt Gingrich restated the long-discredited assertion, "On the economy, the president [George W. Bush] inherited a recession. That's now clear it started in 2000."[22]

Some conservative pundits, like *National Review Online* contributing editor Donald Luskin, argue that NBER is "on the verge of changing the recession's start date" to indicate that the recession began on Clinton's watch.[23]

Luskin made that claim on May 5, 2004, based on a *Washington Post* article from January 2004.[24] Luskin didn't bother mentioning that a more recent *Washington Post* article, from March 2004, had quoted NBER spokesperson Donna Zerwitz saying there was "nothing imminent" about any alleged plans to change the start date.[25]

Regardless of whether Luskin was being honest in ignoring the later *Post* article, it's been nearly seven months, at this writing, since the article he used as his basis for claiming NBER is "on the verge of changing the recession's start date." And it's been three months since Luskin's claim itself. NBER hasn't changed the start date yet.

That's a pretty big "verge."

FEWER JOBS IN 2004 THAN 2000

Crossfire panelist and professional conservative Tucker Carlson is fond of wildly exaggerating liberal positions in order to more easily attack them, to the benefit of conservative Republicans. In response to recent progressive criticism of the Bush economy, Carlson huffed, "The Kerry campaign's attempts to paint the economy as in some great depression are ludicrous. People don't buy them. It's a joke. Actually, it's growing faster than it has in 20 years, and you know it."[26]

Oh, if only just saying something made it true! In reality, the American economy is not growing faster than it has in the past 20 years—far from it.

In January 2001, when President Bush took office, there were 111,560,000 total private-sector jobs; in June 2004, there were 109,762,000. In other words, almost 1.8 million private sector jobs have been lost in the past four years.[27]

Similarly, President Bush is 1.14 million jobs short of the December 2000 total of nonfarm payroll jobs.[28]

Even the better job numbers touted in the first half of 2004 by the president's team have not returned the economy to pre-Bush standards, especially given that there are more and more Americans entering the workforce as they graduate from high school and college:

It is easier for Americans to find work than it was six months ago, but not yet easy. Employers added about 950,000 jobs in the past three months. But that is still 1.3 million shy of the March 2001 peak—and not nearly enough jobs to absorb the 3.4 million people who have joined the labor force since then.[29]

As numerous observers—but few conservative journalists—have noted, jobs have declined during the term of only one other president: Herbert Hoover.[30]

The underperforming U.S. economy has compelled even some prominent conservatives to conclude that the president's policies have not always been in the best interests of the country. "His economists screwed up," Senate Finance Committee Chairman Charles E. Grassley (R-Iowa) said in July 2004, explaining that President Bush was the victim of bad advice when his administration forecast that his tax cuts would create millions of jobs. "[Bush] was not right in not questioning his economists."[50] Grassley's cautious double-negative is confusing. What he is trying to say is that Bush was wrong.

NEW JOBS ARE WORSE JOBS

"[O]n the economy itself and job creation, which is the politically most sensitive part of that, we've had nothing but good news. A half million new jobs created."
—Brit Hume[31]

There must be a "Pollyanna" award being given out to the conservative mouthpiece most willing to spread frosting over the cracks in the Bush economy. That's the only explanation for FOX News anchor Brit Hume's wildly inaccurate claims that "we've had nothing but good news" on the economy and job creation.

In fact, lower- and middle-income households have had a rough go of it because of job displacements, lower-paying job replacements, and wages that have been battered by higher gasoline and food prices. According to a JPMorgan Chase and former Federal Reserve economist:

> To date, the [recovery's] primary beneficiaries have been upper-income households . . . Two of the main factors supporting spending over the past year, tax cuts and increases in [stock] wealth, have sharply benefited upper-income households relative to others.[33]

The same economist estimates that in terms of dollars saved, "the top 20 percent of households by income got 77 percent of the benefit of the 2003 tax cuts, and roughly 50 percent of the 2001 tax cuts."[34]

Average hourly earnings have risen at just a 1.9 percent annual rate since August 2003, whereas the consumer-price index—driven by higher food and gasoline prices—"has risen at a 3.3 percent annual pace." That means that despite the so-called "recovery," weekly earnings for production workers and non-supervisors at service companies, adjusted for inflation, were down 2.6 percent in June 2004 from a year earlier. In other words, the average worker's purchasing power is going *down* despite the "happy face" attitude of Ed Gillespie and numerous conservative journalists.[35]

Despite the rosy economic claims of Hume, Tucker Carlson, and Ann Coulter (See No Evil, Hear No Evil, and Evil, to borrow Bob Dole's famous description of Presidents Gerald Ford, Ronald Reagan, and Richard Nixon), the type of jobs that have been created in the first half of 2004 "have been at the lower end of the economic spectrum."[36]

By industry, the leading sources of recent hiring have been restaurants, temporary hiring agencies, and building services. As Stephen Roach, the Chief Economist at Morgan Stanley, wrote in the *New York Times*:

These three categories, which make up only 9.7 percent of total nonfarm payrolls, accounted for 25 percent of the cumulative growth in overall hiring from March to June. Hiring has also accelerated at clothing stores, courier services, hotels, grocery stores, trucking businesses, hospitals, social work agencies, business support companies and providers of personal and laundry services. This group, which makes up 12 percent of the nonfarm workforce, accounted for 19 percent of the total growth in business payrolls over the past four months.[37]

Again in contrast to the pro-Bush spin propagated by the conservative commentators, "Lower-end industries, which employ 22 percent of the workforce, accounted for 44 percent of new hiring from March to June . . . [F]ully 81 percent of total job growth over the past year was concentrated in low-end occupations in transportation and material moving, sales and repair and maintenance services."[38]

Even worse for the long-range prospects of the American economy, most of the new jobs are part-time jobs and have not benefited the country's full-time workers:

> According to the Bureau of Labor Statistics, the total count of persons at work part-time—both for economic and noneconomic reasons—increased by 495,000 from March to June. That amounts to an astonishing 97 percent of the cumulative increase of the total growth in employment measured by the household survey over this period. By this measure, as the hiring dynamic has shifted gears in recent months, the bulk of the benefits have all but escaped America's full-time workforce.[39]

As we've noted above, George Will callously disregards unemployed American workers and thinks the economy is doing fine. But Will's assurance is little consolation to those who have lost jobs, or have worse jobs than they did a few years ago.

HOURLY AND WEEKLY PAY NOT
KEEPING UP WITH INFLATION

*"It's hard to do it because you gotta look people in the eye and tell
'em they're irresponsible and lazy. And who's gonna wanna do that?
Because that's what poverty is, ladies and gentlemen. In this coun-
try, you can succeed if you get educated and work hard. Period.
Period."*
—Bill O'Reilly[40]

Though O'Reilly claims anyone who works hard will be fine,
USA Today recently noted that many hard-working Americans
have seen their real earning power decrease:

> Over the past year through June, their pay fell 1.1 percent, after
> inflation, according to the Labor Department. By contrast, aver-
> age salaries on Wall Street rose 16 percent last year, one private
> survey shows. A Stanford University economic study found the
> richest 10 percent in the U.S.A. receive 44 percent of all
> income, up from a third in 1980.[41]

This 1.1 percent drop in real earning power is "the steepest
decline since the depths of recession in mid-1991" (during the
presidency of another George Bush, coincidentally) and "came
after a 0.8 percent fall in real hourly earnings in May." In June
2004, production workers were paid an average of $525.84 a
week—after factoring in inflation, that's about $8 *less* than they
made last January.[42]

As noted by an analyst with Economy.com, an independent
provider of economic analysis: "There's more slack than there
appears to be in the labor market . . . Wage growth is still a drag
on overall personal income growth."[43]

The upticks in the economy represent, according to Morgan

Stanley's Stephen Roach, "the weakest hiring cycle" in modern history:

> From the trough of the last recession in November 2001 through last month, private sector payrolls have risen a paltry 0.2 percent. This stands in contrast to the nearly 7.5 percent increase recorded, on average, over the comparable 31-month interval of the six preceding recoveries.[44]

As the economy slowed even more in the second quarter of 2004, consumers were forced to pay higher energy bills and "curbed their spending on just about everything else."[45]

HIGHER JOBLESS RATES FOR MINORITIES

The shaky economic situation in 2004 has been an obvious problem for President Bush, as well as a minefield for right-wing pundits trying either to justify their earlier economic enthusiasm or to uncover a silver lining to buttress the president's popularity.

FOX News Channel contributor Linda Chavez even went so far as to suggest that attempts to alleviate the burdens of poverty are damaging and that minorities benefit from the status quo:

> We are a productive enough country that most people who are in minimum wage jobs are there temporarily. It takes time to climb that ladder, they may be immigrants, and after a few years in this country they'll climb higher, or they may be young people who will move on to better things . . . The problem with raising the minimum wage is if you make the minimum wage beyond what the market really will bear, then you'll end up having employers hiring fewer people, and so you'll have people earning a little bit more money in those jobs, but you'll have fewer of

those jobs. So it ends up hurting people, and it ends up hurting blacks and Latinos the most, and young people.[46]

Chavez is making a bold statement given that the Bush slow-down has been disproportionately harmful to minority workers:

> The weekly earnings for Hispanics and most other workers remain stagnant . . . The median weekly wage for Hispanics has declined in all but one of the past eight quarters. As a result, median wages for Latinos have also lost ground in comparison with the national median wage . . . [J]ob gains did not keep up with population growth.[47]

The struggling economy has also exacerbated the health care shortage among Hispanic Americans. According to an article in the *Wall Street Journal*, "Latinos—the fastest growing population group in the U.S.—were the least likely to have employer cover-age and the most likely to be uninsured."[48]

The economic ravages in the African-American community have been even more devastating, as noted by *New York Times* columnist Bob Herbert: "By 2002, one of every four black men in the U.S. was idle all year long. This idleness rate was twice as high as that of white and Hispanic males." The numbers Herbert referenced did not include those in jail or prison.[49]

PROBLEMS FOR WORKING HOUSEHOLDS

This year, personal consumption spending has slowed to approxi-mately a one percent annual growth rate, the "most sluggish pace since the second quarter of 2001," causing the sales of durable goods (e.g., cars, furniture, and appliances) to fall slightly.[51]

It's also become harder to buy a home, since real estate prices are going up even as wages remain stagnant.

In perhaps the hardest hit of all, health care costs are rising and companies are shifting the burden to workers, as was noted in the *Wall Street Journal*:

> From 2000 to 2003, employees' average annual out-of-pocket expenses for family medical premiums rose 49 percent to $2,412, according to an employer survey by Kaiser Family Foundation, a nonprofit research group in Menlo Park, California.[52]

Given this context, it is not especially surprising to learn that the number of Americans with job-related health benefits "declined to 63 percent from 67 percent between 2001 and 2003." This drop in coverage was unfortunately compounded by a roughly 28 percent increase in health-insurance costs over the two years. The cutback in family benefits is also thought to explain "one of the sharpest drops in employer health coverage"—the 5.3 percentage-point decline among low-income children.[53]

These hardships have caused families to seek "far riskier sources of support" that could further undermine the U.S. economy: "Reliance on tax cuts has led to record budget deficits, and borrowing against homes has led to record household debt. These trends are dangerous and unsustainable, and they pose a serious risk to economic recovery."[54]

But conservatives like Rush Limbaugh are in denial about the burdens on American families, suggesting, "The people that get the minimum wage are not the people Democrats portray them as being—heads of households supporting families of four. It's not the case. Let's get real."[55]

DISCOURAGED WORKERS STOP LOOKING FOR JOBS

Compounding the country's economic problems is the fact that many former workers are not only out of jobs; they have also stopped looking for jobs. Brit Hume may think "we've had nothing but good news" on the economy, but the *New York Times* reported:

Since June 2000, according to the Bureau of Labor Statistics, the number of adults considered "not in the labor force"—those who don't have jobs and are not looking for them—has grown by about 4.4 million, to 66.6 million.[56]

The so-called "labor participation rate"—the percentage of people who are either employed or looking for jobs—has "barely begun to revive" after dropping sharply since 2000. Among adults, ages 25 to 54, the workforce participation rate has dropped to 82.8 percent from 83.9 percent in 2000.[57]

That 82.8 percent is the lowest rate since 1987 and it indicates that millions fewer people are looking for work now. As Edmund Andrews wrote in the *New York Times*:

> In June 2000, the Labor Department estimated that 62.2 million people over the age of 20 were "not in the labor force." By this June, the number had jumped to 66.6 million. The extra 4.4 million amounted to more than half of the 8.2 million people officially labeled unemployed.[58]

PREVIEW OF COMING ATTRACTIONS: SOARING DEFICITS

In 1993, radio right-winger Rush Limbaugh railed against what he called the "dirty little secret" of President Clinton's deficit-reduction plan:

> Though it has been billed as the first meaningful effort at deficit reduction, it's not deficit reduction at all. The administration's own projections show that under the plan the total debt will increase more in four years than it did in any four-year period in the 1980s. Does this seem possible based on what you have heard Clinton and most media analysts say? Yet it's undeniably true. The deficit inherited by Bill Clinton from George Bush was

somewhere around $240 billion. Under Clinton's plan it's going to exceed $300 billion—yet it is called "deficit reduction."[59]

Wrong!

In fiscal year 2001—the last time the federal budget was prepared by the Clinton administration—"there was a surplus of $127 billion."[60]

Soon after President Bush took office in 2001, his budget staff projected a 2004 surplus of $262 billion.[61]

Wrong again!

As of July 2004, the White House projected a budget deficit of $445 billion in this fiscal year—the biggest shortfall ever.[62] Unbelievably, the president's budget director said the $445 billion deficit was good news and that "the improved budget outlook is the direct result of the strong economic growth the president's tax relief has fueled."[63]

Another former fiscal conservative rushing to embrace the Bush deficit was Fred Barnes, who told Brit Hume of FOX News Network:

> It's been projected like $500 billion. Now the projection is something like $400 billion and sinking very fast. I think it could even—by the fiscal year 2005, Bush could have achieved his goal of cutting the deficit in half. And why is it shrinking? Because the economy is growing like crazy, spurred by the tax cuts.[64]

If the economy is growing like crazy, then the Enron scandal was a small accounting error.

There's more on deficits in the next chapter, but there is, sadly, more to discuss about the rest of Bush's economic record.

ADDING INSULT TO INJURY: OUTSOURCING AND ATTACKS ON JOB TRAINING, OVERTIME PROTECTIONS, AND SAFETY LAWS

Outsourcing

Though George Will isn't worried about the decline in U.S.-based manufacturing employment, early this year, President Bush announced that he was appointing Anthony Raimondo, the chief executive of Behlen Manufacturing Company in Columbus, Nebraska, to a new government position designed to help the manufacturing sector of the economy.

It didn't turn out well.

The Bush administration almost immediately came under fire when it was reported that Raimondo "had laid off 75 of his own workers in 2002 after announcing he was constructing a $3 million plant in China." The would-be manufacturing czar defended his operations in China, saying that the Chinese facility did not cause the job losses at his U.S. plants. Raimondo's nomination was withdrawn.[65]

But the cause of outsourcing was taken up by another Bush appointee—the Chairman of the Council of Economic Advisers. In a press briefing, N. Gregory Mankiw said:

> I think outsourcing is a growing phenomenon, but it's something that we should realize is probably a plus for the economy in the long run . . . When we talk about outsourcing, outsourcing is just a new way of doing international trade . . . Outsourcing is sort of the latest manifestation of the gains from trade that economists have talked about at least since Adam Smith.[66]

Move to Eliminate Overtime and Cut Job Training

In early 2004, while workers were struggling to make ends meet in the sluggish economy, the Bush administration issued a new federal regulation making it easier for employers to avoid paying overtime to police officers and firefighters:

Because Bush used the federal regulatory process, the regulation does not require congressional approval . . . According to the Economic Policy Institute, overtime pay accounts for as much as one-quarter of the weekly earnings of workers eligible for overtime. This averages $161 a week . . . Some of the jobs affected are police, firefighters, nurses, retail managers, insurance claims adjusters, and medical therapists.[67]

The year before, the Bush administration proposed cutting funds for job training by nearly $150 million:

The President's budget merges the Employment Service state grants and the *Workforce Investment Act's* adult training and dislocated worker program into one $3.1 billion grant. By consolidating existing programs into larger block grants and redesigning the way job training funds are allocated, the administration threatens to reduce the amount of services available to American workers. Consolidating programs will cut job training spending by $144.4 million and serve 109,000 fewer youths.[68]

Americans are facing real challenges in the Bush economy. There are fewer jobs today than there were four years ago. The jobs that are available aren't as good as the jobs that have been lost. Workers with jobs are getting pay that isn't keeping up with inflation. Many of those without jobs are having so much trouble finding them that they are giving up.

In response, the Bush administration has cut overtime and job training. But conservative pundits don't care. Because they themselves are comfortable, it's easy for them to say everything is fine.

FISCALLY *WHAT?*
Spendthrift Conservatives
and Their Apologists in the Press

"With the continued fiscal discipline of a Republican Congress, we could have federal surpluses for the next 30 years."
—Newt Gingrich[69]

For decades, conservatives have successfully portrayed themselves as fierce guardians of the taxpayer dollar while painting liberals as fiscally irresponsible. Through incessant repetition and anecdotes of dubious origin, conservatives have made the term "tax-and-spend liberal" an accepted fiction.

But conservatives have talked the talk far better than they have walked the walk. The facts show that conservative Republican presidents have played fast and loose with public dollars, while Democratic President Bill Clinton has been the only fiscally responsible (note we didn't say "fiscally conservative": It's time to rid our vocabulary of that false description of budgetary responsibility) occupant of the White House in the past 24 years.

WHITE HOUSE NUMBERS SHOW OUT-OF-CONTROL SPENDING BY CONSERVATIVES

"And the only way to get rid of a deficit is to cut taxes and grow out of it. Every time we've tried that it's happened . . . Well, the Reagan

boom kicked in with those tax cuts in '81 and '82 and all the way through to the mid- to late-'90s, the Reagan boom, and we wiped it out. We had surpluses on paper, didn't we? So you grow your way out of deficits and cuts. And when did this boom start to go south? With the Clinton tax increases, folks! The Clinton tax increases coupled with this phony market bubble, and that's what killed the golden goose."

—Rush Limbaugh[70]

Limbaugh's wrong in so many ways, it's hard to know what to tackle first. Reagan didn't "wipe out" deficits, he increased them. The "Reagan boom" didn't last through the late 1990s, it ended with a recession in the beginning of the decade; the *Clinton* boom in the 1990s (the longest period of economic growth in American history) turned the deficits run up under Reagan and the first President Bush into record surpluses.

According to the White House's own numbers, Bill Clinton has been the only president to control the annual deficit in the past 24 years, while conservatives like Ronald Reagan and George W. Bush have presided over record deficits and runaway spending.

The most startling statistic provided by the White House Office of Management and Budget (OMB) relates to the deficit. From 1980 to the present, four presidents have grappled with the federal budget: three conservative Republicans (Ronald Reagan, George H.W. Bush, and George W. Bush) and one progressive Democrat (Bill Clinton). Despite claims by conservative pundits like Rush Limbaugh, the deficit increased under all three conservative presidents; Reagan doubled the deficit, Bush the elder then nearly doubled it again in his four years, and Bush the younger has exploded the deficit, leaving the American people with the largest annual deficit in our nation's history. The only president in the last quarter-century who truly controlled spending in Washington was William Jefferson Clinton. In fact,

President Clinton left his successor the largest *surplus* in U.S. history, which George W. Bush turned into the largest *deficit* in history in fewer than four years.

DEFICIT DOUBLED UNDER REAGAN: CONSERVATIVE PUNDITS FALSELY BLAME CONGRESS

Limbaugh, like other conservatives, holds Ronald Reagan up as the prime example of financial rectitude, invoking the Gipper as a truly fiscally responsible president. Rhetorically, Republicans like to portray Reagan as stemming the tide of spending in Washington while cutting taxes.

But the numbers show that Reagan just played a budget hawk on television; in real life, he led the country into a deep economic hole. When Ronald Reagan took office in 1981, he inherited a deficit of $73.8 billion. By his third year in office, 1983, the annual deficit had risen to $207.8 billion, an increase of 181 percent, even before he finished his first term.

The deficit reached its Reagan-era high in 1986, when it totaled $221 billion. By the time he left office, Reagan managed to whittle the annual deficit down to $155.2 billion. That total deficit when Reagan left office was double the total deficit when he took office. It doesn't take a trained economist to see that Reagan's record is anything but fiscally responsible. But, just in case, here's what one trained economist, Reagan's own budget director, David Stockman, said of that period: "With the benefit of hindsight, [historians] will know the immense damage to the nation's balance sheet and living standard that resulted from these eight years of fiscal profligacy . . . By then, the secret of the Reagan era's fabulous free lunch will be beyond dispute."[71]

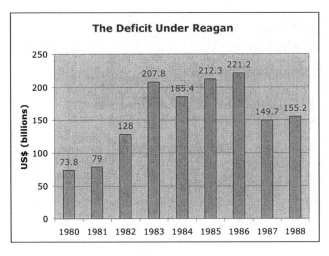

Source: White House Office of Management and Budget

What's worse is that despite the praise he receives from the right for being fiscally prudent, *Ronald Reagan never submitted a balanced budget to Congress.* Instead, he stood by as the annual deficit ballooned out of control. Contrary to Limbaugh's assertion, Reagan's policy did not help the budget "grow out" of a deficit. According to the *Miami Herald*:

> The ballooning debt was the result of Reagan's insistence on slashing tax rates even though he was doubling defense spending—from $157 billion to $304 billion. In his eight years, he never once submitted a balanced budget and the federal deficit averaged almost $200 billion a year.[72]

Contemporary conservatives have tried to shift the blame for Reagan's deficits onto the Democrats in Congress. Their argument is that Reagan wanted to cut spending, but Congress wouldn't let him. Chris Edwards's statement in the *National Review* is a good example:

On spending, Reagan's original February 1981 plan proposed

enough cuts to bring outlays down to 19.3 percent of gross domestic product by 1984 and balance the budget. With a Congress unwilling to make serious cuts, the deficit remained high and spending was stuck at over 22 percent until the late 1980s. With federal spending rising more rapidly than it has in decades, Ronald Reagan's small-government vision is sorely missed in Washington today.[73]

Likewise, columnist Jeff Jacoby claimed,

Far from draining the Treasury, Reagan's policies sent federal revenues surging. The government's take doubled from $517 billion in 1980 to more than $1 trillion in 1990—an inflation-adjusted increase of 28 percent. Unfortunately, spending climbed even faster. Congress routinely declared Reagan's budgets "dead on arrival" and insisted on spending more than he requested.[74]

There's just one problem with this: It isn't true.

Reagan's own budget director placed the blame for deficits at the door of Reagan's White House, calling their economic plan a "reckless, unstable fiscal policy based on the politics of high spending and the doctrine of low taxes."[75] The *Washington Post* noted, upon Reagan's death, "Toward the end of his term, Reagan called the federal budget deficit 'one of my greatest disappointments' and blamed it on congressional reluctance to cut domestic spending, even though the budget proposals he submitted to Congress had not been balanced."[76] But even this was too generous to Reagan; as Al Franken has noted, "Over the eight years of the Reagan presidency, the Gipper asked Congress for $16.1 billion *more* in spending than it passed into law."[77]

Efforts by conservative pundits to blame Congress, rather than Reagan, for the massive deficits of the 1980s are nothing more than revisionist history.

DEFICITS NEARLY DOUBLED
UNDER THE FIRST PRESIDENT BUSH

Next up was George H.W. Bush. When Bush took office, he inherited a deficit of $155 billion. Within 2 years, the deficit was $220 billion again, and heading higher each year. By the end of his four short years, the deficit had nearly doubled, to $290.4 billion in 1992. In 12 years of conservatives in the White House, the deficit had quadrupled. And again, these numbers show that conservative budgets did not somehow "grow out" of a deficit.

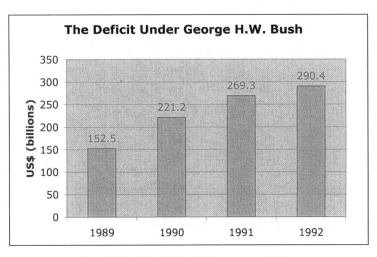

Source: White House Office of Management and Budget

Clinton Created Record Surplus

After 12 years of borrow-and-spend conservative policies, Bill Clinton took office facing a deficit of nearly $300 billion. With some tough political choices, Clinton actually turned the deficit around and created the largest surplus in the history of our country.

What makes the numbers even more impressive is that

Clinton cut the deficit *every year* until he turned it into a surplus in 1998. He handed George W. Bush a $236 billion cushion, the largest in American history.

Despite Clinton's efforts, conservatives were unwilling to admit a progressive president was successfully cutting the deficit. The *Washington Times*' Donald Lambro wrote:

> The GOP's listless and erratic responses to Mr. Clinton's budget have allowed him to get away with murder. He has skillfully cloaked his fiscal policies in the soothing language of balancing the budget, but the five-year reality behind his tax-and-spend plan ensures that government will be much bigger when he's through and the budget will still be in the red.[78]

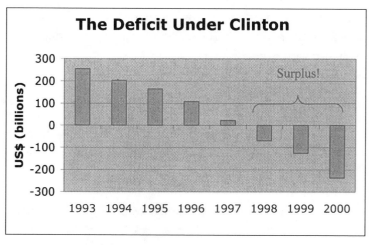

Source: *White House Office of Management and Budget*

White House OMB numbers directly contradict both Lambro's idea that Clinton wasn't truly cutting the deficit and Limbaugh's claim that the deficit "went south" after Clinton raised taxes in 1993. In fact, the deficit *improved* every year after 1993. As you will see, it wasn't until George W. Bush's massive tax cuts for the wealthy that the deficit worsened.

George W. Bush's Legacy: From the Largest Surplus to the Largest Deficit in Just Four Years

When George W. Bush took office in the beginning of 2001, America had a record surplus created by eight years of progressive policies and conservatives had just taken control of all three branches of government. Three and a half years later, conservatives still control the entire federal government—but those record surpluses have turned into record deficits.

The White House Office of Management and Budget has predicted that the annual deficit this year will be $445 billion,[79] the largest deficit in the history of this country.

Of course, conservatives in the media will claim that the budget went into deficit because of the war on terror and the attacks of September 11, 2001, as Sean Hannity did during an exchange with Robert Reich:

REICH: This deficit is out of control.

HANNITY: I agree with you. It is. But you know something? Nine-eleven happened. It had a tremendous impact on the economy.[80]

It isn't just well known partisans like Sean Hannity who make this false claim, however. CNN host Jack Cafferty told viewers, "We had surpluses until September 11, and you know, the war in Iraq and some other things."[81]

But that's just not true: The federal deficit, according to the Congressional Budget Office, went into deficit in August 2001[82]—*before* the terrorist attacks, and *before* the war on terror . . . but *not* before George W. Bush's massive, fiscally irresponsible tax cuts for the wealthy. Not only did the Bush tax cuts (rather than the war on terror) push us into deficit, they account for the largest portion of the deficit to this day, as explained by Citizens for Tax Justice:

• Tax cuts explain most of the debt build-up. Under current policies, the federal government, excluding Social Security, is expected to borrow a total of $10.3 trillion over the fiscal 2002-14 period. More than half of that borrowing—$5.5 trillion—will stem from the President's tax cuts if they are extended.

• The already enacted Bush tax cuts are projected to add $2.6 trillion to the government's debt over the 2002-14 period.

• Extending the tax cuts past their current "sunset" dates, as the President proposes, would more than double the cost of the Bush tax cuts, requiring $2.9 trillion in additional borrowing over the upcoming decade.[83]

While many in the media continue to mislead the public about the causes of the Bush deficits, falsely claiming they were brought about by the terrorist attacks rather than by reckless tax breaks for the wealthy, the facts are clear: We're experiencing massive deficits because George W. Bush cut taxes for the wealthy while increasing spending nearly 30 percent in just four years.

To sum up: Reagan doubled the deficit, Bush the elder nearly doubled it again, and Clinton slashed the red ink and produced a surplus of more than a quarter of a *trillion* dollars. Then, in four short years, George W. Bush returned the country to deficits, this time of record proportions. Far from growing our way out of a deficit, conservative policies have led this country directly into massive debt. It was only under progressive leadership that the country was able to put its financial house in order.

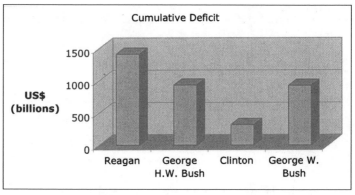

Source: White House Office of Management and Budget

SPENDING INCREASES WERE *SLOWEST* UNDER CLINTON

"You should understand that liberals begin with the belief that the money you and I produce is the government's money . . . Real freedom is only possible by imposing restraints on government."
—Sean Hannity[84]

"Republicans are spending like drunken sailors. But also Democrats spend like drunken sailors . . . You know, liberals are criticizing the president on this, but not only do they spend like drunken sailors themselves, they also tax like drunken sailors."
—Sean Hannity[85]

Despite Sean Hannity's spin about liberals being responsible for runaway government spending, the facts show that of the last four presidents, Bill Clinton kept the tightest control over federal spending, while conservatives like Ronald Reagan and George W. Bush were the ones spending like drunken sailors.

Reagan Increased Outlays By 80 Percent

Of the past four Presidents, Ronald Reagan presided over the largest spending increase. According to White House numbers, Reagan increased government outlays over his eight years by 80 percent. That's right: In just eight years, he nearly *doubled* the size of government. How appropriate, then, that the Ronald Reagan Building in Washington, D.C. is the city's largest federal government building.

George H.W. Bush Increased Spending 29.79 Percent (In Just Four Years)

Reagan's spending binge was followed by George H.W. Bush, who increased spending 29.79 percent. The biggest jump occurred during his second year in office, when he increased spending by more than $100 billion.

George W. Bush Increased Spending 29.62 Percent (In Just Four Years)

George W. Bush comes next, as he has increased spending 29.62 percent. Bush's spending numbers are based on estimated spending for the current year. It should also be noted that any spending for Iraq, which would appear in a supplemental spending bill, could not yet be included in these calculations.

Clinton Presided Over Smallest Spending Increase: 29.46 Percent

Clinton increased spending at the slowest rate, only 29.46 percent during his two terms. While the spending increases under Clinton and both Bushes appear to be similar, it should be noted that Clinton increased spending over 8 years, where both Bushes surpassed his total in only four years.

White House Office of Management and Budget numbers again show that Republicans spent money faster while in the

White House. Second, they show that the conservative hero, Ronald Reagan, spent money the fastest of the last four presidents. Finally, as the chart below shows, OMB numbers demonstrate that Reagan and the two Bushes increased spending more than twice as much as Clinton did.

President	Spending Increase per Year (in billions of dollars)	Spending Increase per Year (percentage)
Ronald Reagan	59.2	10.02%
George H.W. Bush	59.5	7.45%
Bill Clinton	47.4	3.68%
George W. Bush	113.8	7.41%

Source: White House Office of Management and Budget

Clinton Controlled the Size of Government

President Clinton also surpassed his predecessors by imposing restraints on the growth of the federal payroll. Under Bill Clinton, the number of government employees shrunk by 442,804, from 2,226,835 in 1992 to 1,784,032 in 2000. The number of federal employees increased under Reagan and remained relatively static under George H.W. Bush. So it is fair to say that Bill Clinton spent less and cut more from the government than his conservative counterparts.

FISCAL IRRESPONSIBILITY UNDER GEORGE W. BUSH, AND THE PUNDITS WHO LIE ABOUT IT

"We need to be smart about how we spend the money in Washington, D.C. We need fiscal discipline and fiscal sanity. It starts with understanding whose money we spend. We're not spending the government's money in Washington, D.C.; we're spending your money. And you deserve fiscally sound government."
—George W. Bush[86]

"Bush wants fiscal discipline imposed by tax cuts, and I agree."
—Bill O'Reilly[87]

President Bush has signed plenty of tax cuts, mostly for the wealthy. But where's the fiscal discipline that Bill O'Reilly told us comes with tax cuts?

Financial mismanagement of taxpayer dollars has reached its apex during the current era of conservative control of the White House and Congress. Bush and his fellow conservatives have not only returned our nation to deficits, they have put our country further in the red than it has ever been before.

Bush's fiscal record has not gone unnoticed. The Concord Coalition, a bipartisan interest group that advocates fiscal responsibility, has assailed Bush's record. The group, founded by former Republican Senator Warren Rudman and the late Democratic Senator Paul Tsongas, has long argued for balanced budgets and a sound fiscal policy in Washington.

According to many experts, significant responsibility for the current spending lies with this administration and its right-wing cohorts in Congress. Despite spiraling deficits, President Bush has not tried to rein in runaway congressional spending. He has never used his veto pen, which has drawn criticism from fiscally responsible conservatives. As Jeff Birnbaum wrote:

> I know this isn't the season for gift-giving, but I also know that there's one present that George Bush really ought to have: a pen. Not just any pen, a veto pen. Clearly, he doesn't own one. After more than three years in office, he hasn't vetoed a single piece of legislation. Not one. What else can explain the oversight? And given the state of the federal budget these days, the president needs a veto pen with a ribbon wrapped around it.[88]

A few honest conservatives are fed up with his "all talk, no action" approach to fiscal responsibility. Former presidential candidate and deficit hawk John McCain recently took Bush to task for his failure to curb spending in Washington.

> Congress is throwing away astonishing amounts, "spending money like a drunken sailor," and President George W. Bush shares the blame because he is not using his veto power, Sen. John McCain (R-Ariz.) said yesterday.
>
> McCain, an avid critic of spending for lawmakers' pet projects, said the president's reluctance to veto legislation makes it harder for congressional negotiators to kill such spending . . .
>
> He said that spending growth had been capped at 4 percent, but that it was at least 8 percent higher than last year. He said he would continue urging Bush to veto profligate spending bills. The president has not vetoed a single bill since he took office.
>
> Asked if the president bears some responsibility, McCain said: "Yes, because I think that the president cannot say, as he has many times, that 'I'm going to tell Congress to enforce some spending discipline' and then not veto bills."[89]

Bush's inability to rein in the deficit has also spooked business leaders. As the *Los Angeles Times* noted:

> And the very smart people who are worried right now aren't all wet. The burden of driving the global economy may be sapping the U.S. economy's strength as China slows its rampant growth and no other economic engine is on the horizon.
>
> Among the expert worriers is Peter G. Peterson, former Secretary of Commerce and co-founder and chairman of Blackstone Group, the largest private equity investment firm in the U.S. He laid out his fears last week in Los Angeles as he introduced his book *Running on Empty* (Farrar, Straus & Giroux).
>
> Peterson, a lifelong Republican, says rising budget deficits, made worse by continued tax cuts, "could cause global investors

to lose faith" that the U.S. will ever rein in its deficits. And this, he says, "can easily lead to a run on the dollar." Such runs have occurred, he notes, in four separate two-year periods in the last three decades.

Peterson is hardly alone. Investor Warren Buffett, in a special bylined article in March in *Fortune* magazine, bemoaned the fact that U.S. "net worth" is being transferred abroad as Americans must work to pay the interest on the country's net borrowings.

Buffett wrote that for the first time in his investing life, he was placing some of Berkshire Hathaway Inc.'s funds in securities and assets denominated in other currencies.

"To hold other currencies," Buffett wrote, "is to believe the dollar will decline."[90]

In short, Buffett and Peterson believe that deficits are putting our economic health in danger.

Despite conservatives' continued assertion of their budget hawk *bona fides*, there is no evidence that conservative leadership in the White House reduces the budget deficit. To the contrary, whether Congress has been controlled by Democrats or Republicans, it has been Republican presidents who have spent more and created larger deficits. You wouldn't know that from listening to conservative commentators like Rush Limbaugh and Jeff Jacoby, but it's true.

SQUANDERED UNITY
Right-Wing Pundits' Blind Support
for Bush's National Security Policy

THE FICTION OF INTERNATIONAL
HATRED FOR AMERICA

> *"Just before I came on the show, I went and looked up a columnist on the* Arab News, *and he said after September 11, the whole world mourned the death of innocent civilians along with American people. I mean, once again an Arab columnist in the* Arab News, *it's a Saudi paper, perpetuating this, well, it's a fib at best. It just was not true. The very next day, September 12, in almost any country you picked out, you were reading major columnists saying that it was our fault and that we deserved it and that we just didn't get it . . . The entire rest of the world except for 2/3 of Great Britain [said America deserved September 11.]"*
> —FOX News Channel's John Gibson, author of *Hating America*[91]

In January 2004, the *New York Times Magazine's* James Traub noted:

Even some traditional internationalist Republicans believed that the Bush administration had abandoned many of the central tenets of the last several generations of national security policy while squandering much of the global goodwill that came in the aftermath of the terrorist attacks on the World Trade Center and the Pentagon.[92]

Now that the Bush administration has apparently failed to capitalize on the international goodwill the U.S. enjoyed in the aftermath of the September 11 terrorist attacks, his conservative propagandists in the media, like John Gibson of FOX News, are busy claiming the international community was always against us. The rest of the world hates us, they claim, and thought we "deserved" September 11 because they're jealous of us.

Gibson and company know they can't get away with claiming that Bush has successfully won the support of the rest of the world, so they are forced to make the absurd claim that Bush had to go it alone because the rest of the world hates us.

Just how revisionist is this? Gibson claims that "in almost any country you picked out," the newspapers were full of anti-American sentiment on September 12.

September 12, 2003, perhaps.

But on September 12, 2001, the world was united behind us, as expressed by a front-page editorial in *Le Monde*, a French (yes, *French*) newspaper, that day:

> "In this tragic time, when words to express the shock we feel appear meaningless, the first thing that comes to mind is this: We are all Americans," the daily said in a front-page editorial. "We are all New Yorkers, as surely as John Kennedy in 1962 declared in Berlin that he was a Berliner.
>
> "How can we not show—like in the darkest moments of our history—solidarity with this population, with the United States, with whom we are very close and to whom we owe our freedom and thus our solidarity."[93]

British Prime Minister Tony Blair "offered President Bush and the American people our solidarity, our profound sympathy, and our prayers."[94]

French President Jacques Chirac proclaimed:

In these horrifying circumstances, the entire people of France and I want to emphasize this, stand by the people of America. They express their friendship and solidarity in this tragedy. Naturally, I want to assure President Bush of my total support. France, as you know, has always condemned and unreservedly condemns terrorism, and considers that terrorism must be combated by all possible means.[95]

The Germans, too, stood shoulder to shoulder with America, as Chancellor Gerhard Schroeder made clear:

The German people are at the side of the United States of America in this difficult hour. I wish to express my deep-felt condolences and complete solidarity to you and the American people. Our thoughts and prayers go out to the victims and their families.[96]

Even Vladimir Putin, the president of America's Cold War nemesis—Russia—expressed support for the United States:

The event that occurred in the U.S. today goes beyond national borders. It is a brazen challenge to the whole humanity, at least to civilized humanity. Addressing the people of the United States on behalf of Russia I would like to say that we are with you, we entirely and fully share and experience your pain. We support you.[97]

This remarkable international solidarity was short-lived, but it was there. Despite the lies and facile xenophobia right-wing pundits like John Gibson and Bill O'Reilly spout daily, the rest of the world does not hate America—or at least it didn't before George W. Bush appeared to alienate much of it with his unilateral rush into a war based on false pretenses.

It was an important moment in the history of democracy. War

had been declared against the symbol of modern civilization, the United States, and therefore against the idea of civilization itself. Americans were united in a desire for action. The world spoke of its solidarity with us. President Bush had a once-in-a-lifetime opportunity to reshape the world and America's place in it for the better.

But now, conservative commentators try desperately to cover what many see as his failures by sowing distrust of foreigners and telling lies about how the world reacted to September 11.

REPORTERS PLAYED CHEERLEADER DURING THE RUSH TO WAR

How did Bush spend the unprecedented goodwill of the citizens of the United States and leaders around the world? After routing Osama Bin Laden's base country of Afghanistan, Bush did not use the momentum of that action to build a worldwide united front against terror. Instead, he invaded Iraq based on the suspect premises that 1) Iraq was somehow connected to al Qaeda and the attacks of September 11, and 2) Iraq posed an independent and imminent threat to the United States.

The president and his administration forcefully argued that Iraq and Saddam Hussein presented an imminent danger to the American people:

> The regime . . . has aided, trained, and harbored terrorists, including operatives of al Qaeda. The danger is clear: Using chemical, biological or, one day, nuclear weapons, obtained with the help of Iraq, the terrorists could fulfill their stated ambitions and kill thousands or hundreds of thousands of innocent people in our country, or any other.[98]

The claim that Iraq might provide weapons of mass destruction to terrorists gave rise to a second reason to invade Iraq: the imminent danger posed by Iraq itself to the safety of the American people.

> *"They have chemical weapons; they have biological weapons; they're trying to acquire nuclear weapons."*
> —Colin Powell, October 22, 2002[99]

> *"The problem here is that there will always be some uncertainty about how quickly he [Saddam Hussein] can acquire nuclear weapons. But we don't want the smoking gun to be a mushroom cloud."*
> —Condoleezza Rice, September 8, 2002[100]

> *"The threat comes from Iraq . . . It possesses and produces chemical and biological weapons. It is seeking nuclear weapons. It has given shelter and support to terrorism . . ."*
> —George W. Bush, October 7, 2002[101]

The administration's justification for war was tightly scripted, omnipresent, compelling—and false. But the American people had nowhere to go for the truth, as the nation's news media fell for the administration's spin and served as enthusiastic cheerleaders for the pro-war conservatives.

The *New York Times*, in particular, was often an unquestioning supporter of the pro-war position, reporting dubious spin from even more dubious sources as though it were fact. The *Times'* reporting was so uneven, the paper finally (after months of mounting pressure from media watchdogs) acknowledged some of its shortcomings in an extraordinary note from the editors in May 2004:

> We have found a number of instances of coverage that was not as rigorous as it should have been. In some cases, information that was controversial then, and seems questionable now, was insufficiently qualified or allowed to stand unchallenged.

Looking back, we wish we had been more aggressive in re-examining the claims as new evidence emerged—or failed to emerge.

The problematic articles varied in authorship and subject matter, but many shared a common feature. They depended at least in part on information from a circle of Iraqi informants, defectors and exiles bent on "regime change" in Iraq, people whose credibility has come under increasing public debate in recent weeks. (The most prominent of the anti-Saddam campaigners, Ahmad Chalabi, has been named as an occasional source in *Times* articles since at least 1991, and has introduced reporters to other exiles. He became a favorite of hard-liners within the Bush administration and a paid broker of information from Iraqi exiles, until his payments were cut off last week.) Complicating matters for journalists, the accounts of these exiles were often eagerly confirmed by United States officials convinced of the need to intervene in Iraq. Administration officials now acknowledge that they sometimes fell for misinformation from these exile sources. So did many news organizations—in particular, this one . . .

Editors at several levels who should have been challenging reporters and pressing for more skepticism were perhaps too intent on rushing scoops into the paper. Accounts of Iraqi defectors were not always weighed against their strong desire to have Saddam Hussein ousted. Articles based on dire claims about Iraq tended to get prominent display, while follow-up articles that called the original ones into question were sometimes buried. In some cases, there was no follow-up at all.[102]

BEATING DEAD HORSES: REPEATING FALSE JUSTIFICATIONS DOESN'T MAKE THEM TRUE

"Coalition forces, meanwhile, have found further weapons of mass destruction in Iraq."
—Brit Hume, July 2004[103]

No, they haven't.

No weapons of mass destruction have been found. None.

There is no evidence Iraq and al Qaeda had a collaborative relationship. None.

We now know the rationale for going to war was faulty. No weapons of mass destruction have been found. Iraq and al Qaeda did not have a collaborative relationship. But Brit Hume and other conservatives in the media keep right on telling their desperate lies. Hume made his false claim *four days after* U.S. officials announced that the artillery shells in question did not contain chemical weapons after all.

The lies peddled by Hume and other conservative commentators have had an effect: According to a Harris Interactive poll earlier this year, 51 percent of Americans still believe Iraq had weapons of mass destruction when the war began, and 47 percent (a plurality) "believe clear evidence that Iraq was supporting al Qaeda has been found in Iraq."[104] A poll commissioned by *Media Matters for America* in April 2004 found that FOX News viewers were particularly likely to think Iraq had WMD: Among daily viewers of FOX News, 72 percent said there is strong evidence that Iraq possessed WMD and was in the process of developing nuclear weapons.[105]

It is clear that the case for war was false: In mid-2003, the *New York Times* reported that "the chairman of the monitoring group appointed by the United Nations Security Council to track al Qaeda told reporters that his five-member team had found no evidence linking al Qaeda to Saddam Hussein's administration in Iraq."[106]

Likewise, three former Bush administration officials who worked on intelligence and national security issues told *National Journal* that "the prewar evidence tying al Qaeda to Iraq was tenuous, exaggerated, and often at odds with the conclusions of key intelligence agencies."[107]

The bipartisan 9/11 Commission noted "friendly contacts"

between al Qaeda and Iraq and "common themes," i.e., a shared hatred of the U.S. But, according to the commission's final report, "We have seen no evidence that these or the earlier contacts ever developed into a collaborative operational relationship. Nor have we seen evidence indicating that Iraq cooperated with al Qaeda in developing or carrying out any attacks against the United States."[108]

LACKING FACTS, CONSERVATIVES ATTACK

"The rhetoric while we're at war and leading troops in harm's way is reckless and irresponsible."
—Sean Hannity[109]

Leaving aside the obvious rejoinder that the truly "reckless and irresponsible" rhetoric was the conservative spin that enabled a war on false pretenses, putting troops into harm's way, Hannity's comment neatly illustrates the current strategy employed by right-wing commentators. Wrong on the facts and wrong about (recent) history, conservative pundits try to stifle dissent, suggesting that to question the Bush administration's decisions is tantamount to treason. They accuse progressives of "hate" and of being in league with terrorists.

Rush Limbaugh thundered in January 2004, "I can tell you right now that the Democrats will try to exploit everything about Iraq . . . The Democrats are too hate-filled and irrational."[110]

Ann Coulter, author of *Treason: Liberal Treachery From the Cold War to the War on Terrorism*, smeared the entire Democratic Party as extremists: "It's no surprise they want Saddam Hussein back. He made the Democrats seem moderate by comparison."[111]

Conservatives in the media suggest that al Qaeda and other terrorists want John Kerry to defeat George Bush; these outrageous suggestions by a cast of characters including Dick Morris, Oliver North, and Rush Limbaugh have been repeated by more reputable media outlets, including CNN, where reporter Kelly Arena said on air that "[t]here is some speculation that al Qaeda believes it has a better chance of winning Iraq if John Kerry is in the White House."[112] Not only does this speculation lack any basis whatsoever, it ignores one minor detail: According to Reuters, al Qaeda has said it prefers a Bush re-election, noting that it is not possible to find a leader "more foolish" than Bush and that Kerry "will kill our nation while it sleeps." Al Qaeda concluded, "Because of this we desire you [Bush] to be elected."[113]

In the end, playing guessing games about whom terrorists want to win the presidential election is a fool's errand. Terrorists will hate this country no matter who occupies the White House, and whichever candidate becomes president will of course take aggressive action against anyone who threatens our national security. Yet Morris, North, and Limbaugh persist in pushing their speculation on this point.

While asserting that "every terrorist out there is hoping John Kerry is the next president of the United States,"[114] radio host Oliver North also complains, incredibly, that *progressives* have been too partisan: "In the old days, it used to be that when you came to foreign policy, partisan differences ended at the water's edge."[115]

But in lamenting the passage of the good old days, North conveniently ignored that, as a fierce GOP partisan in the late 1990s, he had proudly peddled his own differences with President Clinton regarding Kosovo:

> Apparently the idea of NATO intervention in a sovereign country doesn't bother the impeached Commander in Chief or his Defense Department. But it should bother the Congress. Not just because it establishes a terrible precedent, but because of this administration's terrible record of endless entanglements that keep our sons and daughters in perpetual harm's way.[116]

In 1998, conservative writer and pundit Mona Charen had—to borrow Sean Hannity's words—made "reckless and irresponsible" charges against President Clinton at the very moment when America's enlisted personnel were in harm's way:

> There comes a point beyond which extending the benefit of the doubt becomes foolhardy . . . Bill Clinton . . . proved that there really are no limits to what he will do to save his own hide.[117]

It is this last set of attacks that exposes most clearly the double standard central to the mindset of conservatives. When they question the foreign policy of a president they dislike, they call their anger patriotism. But when others become angry at an administration that led the nation to war on false pretenses, they call *that* anger treason.

Perversely, even while defending the administration's false pretenses for war, conservative pundits have sought to place the blame for the faulty intelligence used by the White House to make the case for invading Iraq on others, as conservative Cal Thomas did in a July 2004 column:

> It is Congress, not the executive branch, that fashions our intelligence apparatus, authorizes money and sets parameters beyond which information collection may not legally go . . . In the matter of Iraq and weapons of mass destruction, Congress had access to the same information given to the White House and the Pentagon. It was information credible to many other nations. In typical hand-washing fashion, Congress now wants to avoid taking the blame and is passing the buck to others.[118]

WHEN ALL ELSE FAILS, DECLARE SUCCESS

President Bush promised to capture Osama Bin Laden "dead or alive."

He hasn't.

Bush diverted our attention to Iraq, and Bin Laden is alive, planning new attacks on American soil.

President Bush declared "Mission Accomplished" in Iraq.

It wasn't.

As of this writing, 784 Americans have died in Iraq since Bush's statement.[119]

But in a striking display of "see no evil, hear no evil" thinking, conservative pundits continue to suggest that things are going well in Iraq and in the war on terror.

Polemicist Ann Coulter denies the disarray and sees the dawn of a political paradise in the Middle East:

> The Americanization of Iraq proceeds at an astonishing pace, the Iraqis are taking to freedom like fish to water, and the possibilities for this nation are endless.[120]

Not content to speak well of the "astonishing" success in Iraq, Coulter also impugns the patriotism of Bush's progressive detractors:

> It's hard to say who's more upset about these developments: the last vestiges of pro-Hussein Baathist resistance in Iraq or John Kerry's campaign manager.[121]

In May 2004, Coulter—always looking for a treasonous conspiracy—also blamed the news media for both the Iraq coverage and the president's weak poll numbers:

> This is the new Tet Offensive. Tet was also a victory, and ABC, NBC, CBS, the *New York Times*, the *Washington Post*, they all said it was a horrible defeat, Walter Cronkite went on TV and said we're in a stalemate . . . The war is going magnificently . . . [W]hy isn't he [President Bush] at like 80 percent? And I think

that is because the media is in campaign mode, like they haven't been since 1992.[122]

In May 2004, when Coulter said the "war is going magnificently," there were 80 American military deaths in Iraq—the second-deadliest month of the war for U.S. troops, following 135 fatalities the month before. Hopefully the men and women of our armed services—and their families—will never experience a war Coulter thinks is going "poorly."[123]

While Coulter believes everything in Iraq has gone swimmingly, MSNBC host (and former conservative Congressman) Joe Scarborough recognizes that isn't the case. Horrifyingly, he doesn't seem to care:

> You can say this of a lot of conservatives I've talked to. They're getting nervous . . . Do they really expect us to win this war and not lose 750, 800, 1,000 American soldiers? Did they really expect us to go into the heart of the Middle East and try to liberate this country without it costing us billions and billions of dollars? I mean, what's with these conservatives?[124]

THE FRIGHTENING IMPLICATIONS OF LOST INTERNATIONAL SUPPORT

America's loss of international support in the three years after 9/11 is—by any standard—startling. And the outrage among allies and other members of the world community is counterproductive to U.S. interests, despite right-wing contempt for "multilateralism" and international coalitions.

Russian leader Vladimir Putin is only one leader who has questioned the United States: "This military action is unjustified . . . There has been no answer to the main question which is: Are there weapons of mass destruction in Iraq and, if so, which ones?"[125]

The Vatican has also been particularly harsh: "Whoever decides that all peaceful means under international law have been exhausted is assuming a grave responsibility before God, his conscience and before history."[126]

The conservative pundit response? Bill O'Reilly claimed papal support for Saddam Hussein, saying, "Theologically, the Pope is on firm ground. Humanistically, he is one of the many Saddam enablers."[127]

International polls have also recorded a precipitous drop in approval for American foreign policy. In early 2004, it was reported that "a majority of people in Canada, Mexico, and five European countries have an unfavorable view of the role that President Bush plays in world affairs." The same poll found that people in Canada, Mexico, and five major European countries "think the war in Iraq increased the threat of terrorism in the world."[129]

The reaction of the conservative media to such international unpopularity is to dismissively mock liberals for valuing multilateral action, as Charles Krauthammer does below:

> The problem with contemporary liberalism is that it believes this nonsense. It sincerely believes that multilateral action—and, in particular, action blessed by the U.N.—is in and of itself morally superior to, and more justifiable than, the United States unilaterally asserting its own national interest.[130]

While there are those like Krauthammer who believe the United States need not worry about the opinions of other nations or their citizens, experts say there are significant policy implications for American unpopularity in the world.

Recent survey data indicates that foreign leaders inclined to support the U.S. are in a political box; because their constituents hold a low opinion of America, leaders are unable or ill inclined to express pro-American positions, as Michael Hirsch noted in *Newsweek*:

So estranged are U.S. relations with many countries that just as the Bush administration is pushing for help from U.N. member states to bolster Iraqi democracy, four members of America's meager coalition have pulled out . . . And Bush and America are so unpopular overseas, polls show, that many foreign leaders can't agree to anything the president asks for without taking a hit in their own ratings.[131]

This loss of international support is complicating the efforts of American officials to hold together the coalition of countries that originally supported the Iraq war, as the *New York Times* observed:

For the first time, administration officials are acknowledging the delicate nature of their "coalition of the willing"—the group of some 30 nations that lent their names and limited numbers of troops to the occupying force built mainly of American and British forces. The multinational force, which the administration stitched together as traditional NATO allies balked, is increasingly tattered.[132]

United States Secretary of State Colin Powell has confirmed the crisis, admitting, "Sure it worries me . . . We've lost some members of the coalition."[133]

The worldwide outcry against U.S. unilateral action has had a final, particularly ominous result, as a Pew poll showed "increased support in Muslim countries for suicide bombings and other forms of violence; 82 percent of Jordanians, 40 percent of Moroccans, 41 percent of Pakistanis and 15 percent of Turks said such violence could be justified."[134]

HAVEN'T THEY DONE ENOUGH?: BUSH'S CUTS TO MILITARY AND VETERANS' PROGRAMS

"For all of Kerry's criticism, Bush has increased veterans and defense spending. Veteran spending is up eight percent per year compared with

three percent under former President Clinton. Defense spending up 10
percent per year compared to one-half of 1 percent under Clinton."
—FOX News Channel's Major Garrett[135]

Garrett's assurances that Bush has increased veterans' funding are misleading. George W. Bush has proposed drastic *cuts* to programs that help our veterans and our active-duty military personnel.

Veterans who have fought and suffered for our country are being forsaken by the Bush administration. In August 2000, presidential candidate George W. Bush told veterans, "The current administration inherited a military ready for the dangers and challenges facing our nation. The next president will inherit a military in decline." He then pledged a $1 billion pay raise for active-duty military personnel, a review of all overseas commitments, a "timely withdrawal" from Bosnia and Kosovo, and $310 million for better schools on or near military bases.[136]

Four years later, administration critics say an overstretched American military is struggling to fight a war without a clear mission or exit strategy.

According to a 2003 report by the Democratic staff on the House Appropriations Committee, the Bush administration last year proposed cuts of about $200 million in the program providing assistance to public schools serving military bases—thus paring education funding "disproportionately for children of soldiers who fought in Iraq."[137]

Other cuts included:

• Failing to extend a child tax credit to nearly 200,000 low-income military personnel.

• A $1.5 billion reduction for military housing and other programs.

• A cut of $14.6 billion over 10 years in benefits paid through the Veterans Administration.[138]

By March 2004, "leaders of veterans' organizations" were voicing "strong criticism of Bush's fiscal 2005 budget plan," complaining that the budget would worsen the backlog in processing disability claims, reduce the number of VA nursing home beds, and force some veterans to pay a fee simply to gain access to the VA health care system.[139]

It was also reported earlier this year that the chairman of the president's veterans' steering committee in New Hampshire had distanced himself from President Bush:

> When the Bush campaign asked James McKinnon to co-chair its veterans' steering committee in New Hampshire—a job he held in 2000—the 56-year-old Vietnam veteran respectfully, but firmly, said no.[140]

According to McKinnon, who served two tours in Vietnam with the Coast Guard, "I basically told them I was disappointed in his support of veterans . . . He's killing the active-duty military . . . Look at the reserves call-ups for Iraq, the hardships. The National Guard—the state militia—is being used improperly. I took the president at his word on Iraq, and now you can't find a single report to back up or substantiate weapons of mass destruction."[141]

Sixteen months after President Bush declared "Mission Accomplished" in Iraq, American combat fatalities continue to increase. And then there's the personnel shortage at the U.S. Army, which has been forced to recall many personnel to active duty—including at least 15 musicians.

You read that correctly: musicians.

Congressman Vic Snyder of Arkansas asked the Army why it needed the 15 musicians.

The answer, according to Snyder: The musicians were being called up to play at military funerals.

In May 2003, right after President Bush declared "Mission

Accomplished," conservative commentator Michael Savage pronounced:

> President Bush's speech aboard the USS Abraham Lincoln was one of the finest moments of his presidency and a great moment for this country.[142]

As recalled musicians play at the funerals of American service members, right-wing pundits' continued focus on the triumphal imagery pushed by this conservative administration seems far out of place.

BAD MEDICINE
How Right-Wing Pundits
Can Really Make You Sick

THE UNINSURED: CONSERVATIVES SUPPORT COR-PORATIONS, PROGRESSIVES SIDE WITH PATIENTS

"If choice is good everywhere in the economy, why wouldn't it be good in health care, as it is in practically any other area of the economy?"
—Rush Limbaugh[143]

"So just look, you know, hotel rooms are priced on what various elements of the economy can afford to pay. That's why there's Super 8, Motel 6, Best Western, all the way up to, take your pick. But in health care there's no concern for whether or not a patient can afford anything . . ."
—Rush Limbaugh[144]

While a stratified market is acceptable for commodities like shoes, cars, or hotels, such a market, in which only a few can afford the best treatment, is neither ideal nor even acceptable for health care.

The contrast between the conservative health care thinking represented by Limbaugh's statements and the statistical evidence regarding the achievements of progressive policy could not be sharper. While progressive thinkers examine difficult issues through the lens of solid scientific thinking and then propose policies that will have a significant positive impact on the health of American citizens, conservatives choose to emphasize ideology rather than effectiveness.

Skyrocketing prices have put health insurance out of reach for many Americans. The price of health care continues to increase far faster than the rate of inflation. In 2003, health care costs rose 14.7 percent (versus an inflation rate of less than 3 percent) and are expected to rise another 12.4 percent in 2004.[145] Last year, 86 percent of employees had to make a higher contribution to their health coverage program costs and 72 percent faced higher deductibles.[146]

While the conservatives insist that there is nothing the government can do to fix the health care crisis and that the array of "choices" offered by a free market is sufficient, those "choices" remain out of reach for many families without government assistance. The Children's Health Insurance Program (CHIP), signed into law by President Clinton in 1997, has made a tremendous impact by reducing the number of children without health insurance. As private coverage has become increasingly unaffordable for working families with children, the CHIP program has provided a safety net. As a result, the percentage of children uninsured for more than a year decreased from 8.4 percent in 1997 to 5.3 percent in 2003.[147]

Throughout the Clinton administration, conservatives in Congress repeatedly blocked efforts to expand access to health care beyond the CHIP program. As a result, despite a strong economy during the '90s, the overall percentage of uninsured Americans hovered around 16 percent.[148]

Unfortunately, conservatives' dependence on money from pharmaceutical companies and the health insurance industry, and the GOP's resulting resistance to reforms to the health care system, have stymied progressive efforts to lower health care costs and reduce the number of uninsured Americans. And big drug and insurance companies knew they would have an advocate in George W. Bush:

In the thick of the 2000 presidential campaign, executives at Bristol-Myers Squibb, one of the nation's largest drug companies, received an urgent message: donate money to George W. Bush.

The message did not come from Republican campaign officials. It came from top Bristol-Myers executives, according to four executives who say they donated to Mr. Bush under pressure from their bosses. They said that they were urged to donate the maximum—$1,000 in their own name and $1,000 in their spouse's—and were warned that the company's chief executive would be notified if they failed to give.

Bristol-Myers said no one was forced to donate. But elsewhere in the drug industry, the message about the election was much the same. At some companies, officials circulated a videotape of Vice President Al Gore railing against the high price of prescription drugs. A torrent of contributions for Mr. Bush and other Republicans resulted. And the money kept flowing, right through the elections of 2002.

Those donations may soon pay off handsomely for the pharmaceutical business. Four years ago, a Democrat was in the White House and the industry was bitterly fighting a prescription drug proposal that it said would have led to price controls. Today, a Republican-controlled Congress is preparing to send a Republican president a measure with a central provision—the use of private health plans to deliver Medicare prescription drug benefits—that is tailor-made to the industry's specifications.[149]

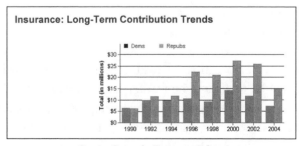

Source: Center for Responsive Politics

Drug companies have also spent millions on advertising campaigns to influence federal health care policy. To note just one example, during the 2000 election cycle, Citizens for Better Medicare (an arm of the pharmaceutical industry) aired more television commercials after Super Tuesday than any other organization except the two political parties (the group's ads constituted 27 percent of non-party ads). The group was also the biggest sponsor of non-party ads aired in the last two months of the election (20 percent of non-party ads).[150]

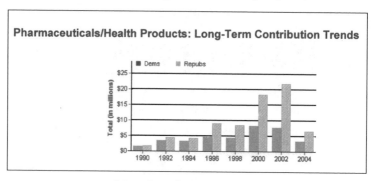

Source: Center for Responsive Politics

"SOME FORM OF COVERAGE" IS NOT ENOUGH ON PRESCRIPTION DRUGS

"Seventy-six percent of American seniors already have some form of prescription drug coverage. All this you've heard about this being a pressing entitlement, it's either dog food or medicine, or it's starvation or medicine, have you heard this? It's BS."
—Rush Limbaugh[151]

When Rush Limbaugh starts talking about food and medicine, we're tempted to defer to him. After all, he's an expert on both.

But he's also wrong. He's wrong to suggest that, because 76 percent of seniors have "some form of prescription drug coverage," there isn't a problem. What's important isn't whether most seniors have "some form of prescription drug coverage." What's important is that all seniors—*all Americans*—have access to the medication they need.

"Some form of prescription drug coverage" isn't the goal, it's just a tactic for reaching that goal—and a pretty vague tactic, at that. But our seniors don't need tactics. They need medicine, and they need food. And they shouldn't have to choose between the two.

If Rush Limbaugh believes that seniors have ready access to the drugs they need, perhaps that's because he's had *too much* access to prescription drugs.

Limbaugh claims that 76 percent of seniors have coverage, but in 2001, only 34 percent of non-institutionalized Medicare beneficiaries had employer-sponsored benefits (28 percent as retirees). Twenty-three percent owned a Medigap policy, but only seven percent of all beneficiaries had drug coverage from Medigap. And because of gaps in Medicare's coverage, the elderly spent an estimated 22 percent of their income, on average, for health care services and premiums in 2002.[152]

The real question for Mr. Limbaugh is: What does "some form of prescription drug coverage" mean? Republicans have been touting the benefits of their "Medicare discount card" when it has been shown to be little more than a sham:

> Bush administration officials and Republicans in Congress struggled to get out the message that the cards could save 10 percent to 25 percent off retail prices for consumers with no drug coverage. Prices, they say, have already come down since the government began posting comparative data on a website (www.medicare.gov).
>
> But Democrats said the prices available with the Medicare cards were often considerably higher than those charged by drugstores in Canada, where government agencies regulate drug prices.
>
> PharmacyChecker.com, an independent evaluator of mail-

order and online pharmacies, reached a similar conclusion. By shopping at some of the licensed Canadian pharmacies listed on its website, the company said, consumers can often buy drugs for less than by using Medicare cards.[153]

For 15 million low-income Medicare beneficiaries, the situation is even worse. For Medicare beneficiaries with incomes over 175 percent of poverty level, only 45 percent have drug coverage through an employer-sponsored plan. For those with incomes under 175 percent of poverty, the number with employer-sponsored drug coverage drops to only 15 percent.[154]

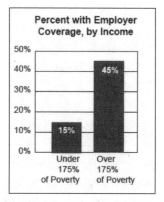

Source: Families USA, Low-Income Medicare Beneficiaries Are Most in Need of Prescription Drug Coverage Fact Sheet

That doesn't stop conservative pundits like Tucker Carlson from downplaying the problem. Carlson has suggested that few Americans have trouble paying for prescription drugs: "If you look at the surveys of people who actually need money for prescription drugs, there's not some huge percentage of Americans who can't pay the prescription drug bills."[155]

Conservative pundits like Carlson may feel the need to downplay the prescription drug problem because the plain text of the Bush administration's prescription drug plan shows it will do little to help low-income Medicare beneficiaries. Not only does the Bush plan actually encourage employers to drop their coverage of prescription drugs for retirees, it includes a punitive asset test that will deny crucial drug subsidies to 2.8 million very low–income seniors. Low-income seniors with as little as $6,000 in assets would be denied extra help paying for their prescriptions.[156]

PLAYING POLITICS WITH STEM CELL RESEARCH

> *"The left is so transparent: Nobody ever heard of this incredibly important research on human embryos until 10 minutes ago. Yet everyone makes believe he's known about the undiscovered bounty in human embryos forever, and talks about it with real moral indignation."*
> —Ann Coulter[157]

> *"So what great advance are we to expect from experimentation on human embryos? They don't know. It's just a theory."*
> —Ann Coulter[158]

Stem cell research provides a clear lesson in the different ways the left and right approach complex health care issues. While progressives have formulated policy by trying to understand the real science behind stem cells, conservatives like Coulter have refused to engage in true debate, choosing instead to baldly assert that stem cell research has no value, while pandering to their political allies. The conservative choice to consider this issue solely through a political lens while demonizing experts who disagree with them has unfortunately become national policy.

In November 1998, a team of scientists at the University of Wisconsin published the results of their work on stem cells in the journal *Science*. Their 17 years of research in this critical field demonstrated the healing potential of stem cells:

By providing the raw material for virtually every kind of human tissue, new customized strategies for treating a wide range of human diseases including diabetes, heart disease, some forms of cancer, and Parkinson's disease can now be developed.[159]

In testimony before a Senate committee, Dr. Harold Varmus, Director of the National Institutes of Health, said, "It is not too unrealistic to say that this research has the potential to revolutionize the practice of medicine and improve the quality and length of life . . . There is almost no realm of medicine that might not be touched by this innovation."[160]

Despite conservatives' claims that the science behind stem cell research is unsound, scientists themselves disagree. According to the University of Wisconsin stem cell research project:

There is no doubt among biologists that embryonic stem cells have vast potential. There are no other cells that can perform the same biological feats as embryonic stem cells. They can morph into any one of the 220 types of cells and tissues in the human body. Nurtured in their undifferentiated state, they can proliferate endlessly in culture, and provide a vast supply of cells for research and, someday, therapy. And perhaps most importantly of all, they provide our only window to the earliest stages of human development and, after differentiation, access to more specialized cells that could vastly improve our understanding of the onset of cell-based diseases, and perhaps ways to prevent them.[161]

After the University of Wisconsin's announcement, President Clinton requested a review of the issues surrounding stem cell research by the National Bioethics Advisory Commission, a committee appointed by the president to advise the federal government on bioethics issues. In September 1999, the committee released its report, concluding that the federal government should fund both research on and the derivation of human ES cells, provided that only embryos leftover from fertility treatments were used. It proposed that Congress carve out an exception to its embryo research ban for the derivation of embryonic stem cells. In August 2000, the National Institutes of Health, with the support of President Clinton, solicited applications for its first stem cell research grants.[162]

But while President Clinton recognized the tremendous life-saving potential of this issue and based his policies on the guidance of experts in both science and ethics, as a candidate for president, George Bush was focused only on the politics of the issue.

> [S]tem-cell research is a "lightning rod issue," [Patrick] Kelly [a representative of the national Biotechnology Industry Organization] said, partly because the two men who are vying for the White House differ so deeply over it.
>
> Gov. George W. Bush, under intense pressure from abortion opponents in Congress and around the nation, opposes research on cells taken from human embryos. He has called instead for studies involving adult cells.[163]

After becoming president, Bush reiterated his opposition to stem cell research to the Culture of Life Foundation, a pro-life organization whose Board of Directors includes former Republican presidential candidate Alan Keyes.

Bush maintains his position despite strong opposition from those fighting disease. Advocacy groups, including the Juvenile Diabetes Foundation, the Parkinson's Action Network, the National Coalition for Cancer Research, and the National Coalition on Spinal Cord Injury, have joined together to form the Coalition for Advancement of Medical Research to the President. The Coalition works to alter the administration's current policy that severely limits stem cell research.

THE WHITE HOUSE
WASHINGTON

May 18, 2001

Mr. Robert A. Best
President
The Culture of Life Foundation, Inc.
Suite 1111
815 15th Street, N.W.
Washington, D.C. 20005-2256

Dear Mr. Best:

Thank you for your letter about the important issue of stem cell research.

I share your concern and believe that we can and must do more to find the causes and cur
diseases that affect the lives of too many Americans.

That's why I have proposed to double funding for National Institutes of Health medical r
on important diseases that affect so many American families, such as breast cancer. My p
represents the largest funding increase in the Institutes' history. I also have called for an
of the Research and Development tax credit to help encourage companies to continue res
life-saving treatments.

I oppose Federal funding for stem-cell research that involves destroying living human em
support innovative medical research on life-threatening and debilitating diseases, includir
research on stem cells from adult tissue.

We have the technology to find these cures, and I want to make sure that the resources ar
as well. Only through a greater understanding through research will we be able to find cu
will bring new hope and health to millions of Americans.

Sincerely,

George W. Bush

Since President Reagan's death due to Alzheimer's Disease, the issue of stem cell research has gained prominence, but not enough to suggest that any change in the current administration's policy is likely. The right-wing base of the Republican Party, which opposes this potentially life-saving research, has far too strong a hold on President Bush for him to change his mind.

Conservative pundits will even attack their own royalty for opposing them on this issue. Regarding Nancy Reagan's support of stem cell research, Ann Coulter says:

Someone persuaded poor, dear Nancy Reagan that research on human embryos might have saved her Ronnie from Alzheimer's. Now the rest of us are supposed to shut up because the wife of America's greatest president (oh, save your breath, girls!) supports stem cell research . . .

But you can't blame Nancy. As everyone saw once again last week, she's still madly in love with the guy. She'd probably support harvesting full-grown, living humans if it would bring back Ronnie.[164]

To satisfy Bush's political base, the administration has gone so far as to politicize what are supposed to be non-partisan scientific advisory appointments. In February 2004, Bush dismissed Dr. Elizabeth Blackburn, a leading cell biologist, and Dr. William May, a prominent medical ethicist, from the President's Council on Bioethics. The Council is charged with advising the president on the ethical implications of advancements in biomedical research, including stem cell research. Dr. Blackburn, who had served for three years, was removed from the panel soon after she objected to a Council report on stem cell research. She believes she was dismissed because she disapproved of the Bush administration's restrictive position on stem cell research and because she and Dr. May frequently disagreed with the administration's positions on the ethics of biomedical research.[165]

In place of the two panel members who were dismissed, Bush named three replacements, all of whom were vocal supporters of the administration's position on the issue, as was noted in the *Washington Post*:

President Bush yesterday dismissed two members of his hand-picked Council on Bioethics—a scientist and a moral philosopher who had been among the more outspoken advocates for research on human embryo cells.

In their places he appointed three new members, including

a doctor who has called for more religion in public life, a political scientist who has spoken out precisely against the research that the dismissed members supported, and another who has written about the immorality of abortion and the "threats of biotechnology."[166]

Complex issues such as stem cell research deserve better than politics-first thinking and the marginalization of important voices in the debate. Unfortunately, conservatives refuse to discuss stem cell research across the full range of issues involved.

ALL TALK, NO ACTION: CONSERVATIVES ON HIV/AIDS

"Do you see the Democrats [sic] *anything other than sheer hatred for Bush? . . . He has given them more than they've ever spent or even proposed on AIDS research."*
—Rush Limbaugh[167]

Limbaugh's assertion that Bush has done more to stop the spread of HIV/AIDS is demonstrably false. By comparison to the record increases in funding made by the Clinton administration, Bush's policy looks like nothing short of neglect. From fiscal year 1995 to 2001, the average annual increase in federal HIV/AIDS spending was 19.3 percent. From fiscal year 2002 through 2004, the average increase has been only 4.3 percent— barely more than the average inflation rate of 2.3 percent over the same period.

Bush's failure to support proper funding levels comes at a cost. A coalition of health care, religious, and civil rights organizations, the National Organizations Responding to AIDS (NORA), notes:

Unfortunately, HIV/AIDS funding levels in key prevention and care programs have stagnated over the past few years. As a result, previous decreases in the rates of new HIV infections have stopped. Waiting lists for anti-HIV medications and specialized medical care have increased—a snapshot taken in February 2003 found 16 states had restrictions on their federally supported AIDS Drug Assistance Programs (ADAP), a component of the Ryan White CARE Act.

Funding cuts are now forcing the communities hardest hit by HIV to cut medical and dental care, food delivery programs, and substance abuse treatment.[168]

Indeed, President Bush's budget request for fiscal year 2004, as in years prior, falls more than a billion dollars short of meeting the need for HIV/AIDS prevention, care, and treatment.

Program	NORA Recommendation	Bush Budget Request	Difference
Minority HIV/AIDS Initiative	$610 million	$407 million	-$203 million
CDC HIV Prevention & Surveillance	$1.3 billion	$695.9 million	-$604.1 million
CDC STD Prevention	$342.6 million	$168.2 million	-$174.4 million
Ryan White CARE Act	$2.445 billion	$2.08 billion	-$365 million
Indian Health Service HIV/AIDS programs	$10 million	$4.1 million	-$5.9 million
NIH Office of AIDS Research	$3.135 billion	$2.93 billion	-$205 million
Office of HI/AIDS Policy	$2 million	$0	-$2 million
Housing for People with AIDS (HOPWA)	$350 million	$294.8million	-$55.2 million
President's Emergency Plan for AIDS Relief	$3.6 billion	$2.8 billion	-$800 million

Source: NORA Fiscal Year 2005 HIV/AIDS Appropriations Recommendations

Since President Bush took office in 2001, his budget requests for AIDS programs have essentially been flat. In his first budget, he proposed no new funding for care and treatment programs under the Ryan White Act, and virtually no new funding for CDC prevention programs—a mere one percent increase.[169] In Bush's most recent budget, proposed funding for HIV/AIDS programs is again flat, including just one percent more for treatment and care and .001 percent more for prevention.[170] Clearly, more could be done to prevent the 40,000 new HIV infections that occur in the U.S. each year and to treat the 850,000 to 950,000 U.S. residents living with HIV infection.[171]

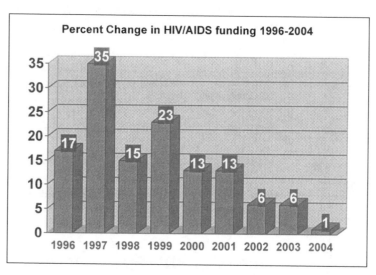

Source: Kaiser Family Foundation, Trends in U.S. Government Funding for HIV/AIDS

Bush's unwillingness to adequately support HIV/AIDS programs is likely met with approval by his conservative chorus, who, if Rush Limbaugh is any indicator, apparently don't care about the impact of AIDS because they don't believe heterosexuals are affected:

And remember, back then in the '80s, one of the accompanying—

there—there—there—there was a lot of fear-mongering going on around—about AIDS, as a lot of people were scared about it. And one of the things that—that the—the AIDS activists said regularly back then was, oh, this is only a matter of time before it spreads to the heterosexual community. It's only a matter of time.

And they used that as—as one of the weapons to try to get people like Reagan to start talking about it from their standpoint. And of course it—it hasn't. It—it didn't, and it hasn't, other than in Africa, and in Africa it is—it is being spread not just by—it—it—it's promiscuity that—that—that spreads this, if you want to know the truth. It's promiscuity.

But it—it hasn't made that jump to the heterosexual community.[172A]

Despite Limbaugh's claims that AIDS doesn't affect heterosexuals, statistics from the Centers for Disease Control and Prevention's Division of HIV/AIDS Prevention show that as of December 2002, an estimated 135,628 Americans had been diagnosed with AIDS as a result of heterosexual contact.[172B] The U.S. Department of Health and Human Services' January 2004 "Facts and Figures" shows that, of new infections in the United States, 15 percent of men and 75 percent of women with AIDS were infected through heterosexual sex.[172C]

MEDICAL MALPRACTICE:
THE FALSE PROMISE OF TORT REFORM

"Medical malpractice reform is moving steadily through Congress . . . The administration is hoping the reforms will head off a national malpractice crisis, which has already closed emergency rooms and trauma centers in Philadelphia and Las Vegas and sent doctors out on strike in Texas, West Virginia, and New Jersey. Obstetricians are particularly affected by rising premiums for malpractice insurance, and in many states it is getting difficult to find doctors who will deliver babies."
—William Tucker[173]

Polls consistently show Americans rank health care and its resulting costs near the top of the nation's priority list. But instead of offering solutions to address the high cost of health care, conservatives have cynically preyed on the public's need for lower health care costs, using the crisis as an excuse to push one of their pet issues, tort reform.

Conservatives claim health care costs too much not because insurance companies gouge their customers or prescription drug manufacturers charge patients the highest prices in the world for products that the American taxpayer has already paid to develop. Rather, they claim, the fault lies with trial lawyers, who put doctors out of business with lawsuits. Their thinking seems to be that we shouldn't blame doctors who commit malpractice for their resulting high insurance costs; we should instead blame the justice system that holds them responsible. Apparently, the conservative mantra of "personal responsibility" doesn't apply to the health care industry that so generously funds conservative causes. Trial lawyers make an easy target, but it's hard to see why they are more responsible for health care costs than insurance companies and drug manufacturers.

Of course, what makes the conservative attacks on lawyers so successful is that there is a germ of truth. There are, indeed, many doctors who face steep increases in their malpractice insurance premiums through no fault of their own. The question is how to fix the problem; how to ensure that good doctors are not driven out of the profession by increased costs, while ensuring that health care providers are held accountable for their mistakes, *and* while keeping costs under control. President Bush and the conservatives think (as usual) the answer is tort reform, and have been pushing to limit the noneconomic damages that can be awarded if someone sues a doctor. That change alone, they claim, will lower the premiums for doctors and end the health care crisis as we know it.

They're wrong, of course—and if they've studied the issue, they must know they're wrong. Maybe they just don't care, because their proposed solution allows them a way to achieve their long-held goal of tort reform.

Punitive damages are awarded in less than one percent of medical malpractice cases[174] and only five percent of doctors (one out of 20) are responsible for 54 percent of malpractice insurance payouts.[175] More importantly, in states that have already limited awards for malpractice, *there has been no decrease in the medical malpractice insurance premiums doctors pay.*

That's an important point, and worth repeating: Despite conservatives' claims that limiting malpractice awards will cause doctors' insurance premiums to go down, *that hasn't happened* in states that have already limited malpractice awards.

Both the Missouri Department of Insurance and the Kentucky Legislative Research Council have recently issued reports suggesting that capping punitive damages would have little effect on physicians. The latter noted:

> There was no evidence that premiums were lower when noneconomic damages are capped . . . Caps on punitive damages resulted in higher premiums for internists and general surgeons and fewer physicians in total for all three specialties.[176]

These findings are consistent across almost all of the states that have enacted medical malpractice caps, as detailed in a 2003 study from Weiss Ratings:

> [A]mong the 19 states with caps, only two of the states, or 10.5 percent, experienced flat or declining med mal premiums. In contrast, states without caps were actually better able to contain premium rate increases, with six, or 18.7 percent, experiencing stable or declining trends.

Tort reform has failed to address the problem of surging medical malpractice premiums, despite the fact that insurers have benefited from a slowdown in the growth of claims. The escalating medical malpractice crisis will not be resolved until the industry and regulators address the other, apparently more powerful, factors driving premiums higher.[177]

Looking at medical malpractice from the total federal level, rather than state by state, leads to the same conclusion. Malpractice simply isn't a large enough portion of overall health care spending for its limitation to make an impact on total health care costs, as a 2004 Congressional Budget Office report found:

> Malpractice costs amounted to an estimated $24 billion in 2002, but that figure represents less than 2 percent of overall health care spending. Thus, *even a reduction of 25 percent to 30 percent in malpractice costs would lower health care costs by only about 0.4 percent to 0.5 percent,* and the likely effect on health insurance premiums would be comparably small.[178]

There is simply no real-world reason to believe that capping malpractice awards will result in a significant decrease in health insurance costs. But you couldn't learn that by listening to the conservative pundits and commentators who choose to ignore the mathematics of malpractice caps. Sean Hannity exemplified the right's head-in-the-sand approach in a conversation with former Gore campaign advisor Richard Goodstein:

> GOODSTEIN: The Congressional Budget Office said that these bills that would cap noneconomic damages at $250,000, if enacted, would increase by—would basically save only 0.4 percent of the amount that's spent now.
> We're really not talking about anything that has a macro, a major influence on the cost of health care . . .

HANNITY: Do you know how silly your statement is when you say there's no major impact on the cost?

Just the cost of malpractice insurance alone for doctors in the last 25 years in this country, because of trial lawyers' suits, has driven up the cost of health care astronomically.

Go look at—just talk to the average doctor. I have all people in medicine in my family. I know the costs.[179]

Faced with facts—actual studies with actual empirical conclusions and statistics—Hannity falls back on an old schoolyard standby: He dismisses them as "silly."

The failure of malpractice caps to regulate insurance costs should, in the end, come as no surprise, as the insurance industry has clearly stated it has no plans to cut insurance premiums even if Congress were to pass restrictions on damages awards. In a press release, the American Insurance Association stated: "[T]he insurance industry never promised that tort reform would achieve specific premium savings."[180]

This is not a problem that can be solved when conservatives pass the buck from insurers, whose profit motive drives high costs throughout the system, to the weakest participants in the health care system, patients.

Conservatives' blind eye to the health care crisis in this country has left many citizens struggling with the costs of health insurance and prescription drugs. Conservative dogmatism is preventing crucial research on using stem cells to cure disease and setting back progress that has been made in HIV/AIDS funding. The right's primary solution to the health care crisis is a limit on malpractice awards, which, despite Sean Hannity's insistence that his family is representative of the entire medical industry, likely would have little impact on health care costs.

MISEDUCATION
The Conservative Media's Smoke Screen
Around Right-Wing Attacks on Public Schools

A public education for all our nation's children, no matter where they live, no matter what their parents do for a living, and no matter what the color of their skin, has long been considered fundamental to our notion of what it is to be an American. In 1865, President Abraham Lincoln spoke of the reconstruction of the South in the aftermath of the Civil War, and the people of Louisiana who had "sworn allegiance to the Union . . . [and] organized a state government, adopted a free-state constitution, giving the benefit of public schools equally to black and white."[181] Support for public education has not always been a partisan issue, but with the advent of the Gingrich Revolution in 1994, conservatives have turned against our nation's schools. After unsuccessful attempts to eliminate the Department of Education entirely, they have since set about trying to starve it to death.

DOING THE MATH ON EDUCATION FUNDING:

"Today, 2003, the federal budget is over 2.2 trillion, and of that 2.2 trillion, how many of you know what we're spending on education? I know a lot of you think that it's not enough. We're spending $745 billion, and actually that number is 2001-2002. We spend $300 billion

a year on defense, the defense of the country, for crying out loud. We're spending close to three times that on education."
—Rush Limbaugh[182]

Limbaugh's erroneous statement is a sad but powerful indictment of conservative thinking about public education. While liberals have persistently sought solutions to the challenges of America's public schools, conservatives seek to disengage from this crucial responsibility. As a result of their distance, they sometimes get their facts wrong. Let's start with Limbaugh.

First of all, his math is bad, which perhaps is an indication that we aren't spending enough on education. $300 billion times three would be $900 billion, not $745 billion.

Second, the federal government does not spend $745 billion on education. The federal government doesn't spend $700 billion, or $600 billion, or $500 billion on education. The federal government doesn't spend even $100 billion on education. No, in 2004, according to the Department of Education, federal education spending comes to $63.3 billion—less than one-tenth of what Limbaugh claimed.

Limbaugh was simply lying.

Limbaugh said we spend $745 billion "of that 2.2 trillion"—which would be about a third of the federal budget—on education. Instead, less than three percent—*three*, not *thirty*—of the federal budget goes to education.

Limbaugh was simply lying.

Limbaugh said the federal government spends nearly three times as much on education as on defense. In fact, the federal government spends about five times as much on defense as on education.

Limbaugh was simply lying. Why? *Because that's what he does.*

THE CONSERVATIVE ATTACK ON PUBLIC EDUCATION

Spending Cuts:

While conservative writer John Podhoretz would have us believe that "[Bush] has imposed a new doctrine of accountability on the American educational system,"[183] the right-wing's education policy has been shown to be an ongoing attempt to cut or otherwise shortchange public education.

When conservative Republicans took control of Congress in 1995, one of their first attempted actions was to eliminate the Department of Education. The House budget proposed abolishing the Department of Education (along with the Departments of Commerce and Energy) and would have eliminated the Corporation for Public Broadcasting, the home of *Sesame Street* and other educational programming, as well as 13 other agencies. The budget passed the House with all but one Republican vote.[184]

Newt Gingrich's ultra-conservative leadership team also pushed for deep *retroactive* cuts in education programs. The rescissions bill passed in the first three months of 1994 slashed funds from education programs: $148 million from reading, writing, and math programs for disadvantaged children, $16 million from aid to schools in areas with military bases (that aid offset the lack of local revenue used for schools), $167 million from the Pell Grant program and other college scholarships, $119 million from vocational and adult education programs, $27 million from school library programs, and $471 million from the Safe and Drug Free Schools program—effectively eliminating it.[185]

Vouchers:

"School vouchers make a big difference for black students. That is the conclusion of a two-year study in three cities—New York,

*Washington and Dayton, Ohio—conducted by a team from Harvard,
the University of Wisconsin and the Brookings Institution. These are
not hotbeds of right-wing ideology. The improved test performance of
African-American students who were able to take advantage of
vouchers suggests a stunning reversal of their fortunes. If the trend
line continues, the report says, 'the black-white test gap could be eliminated in subsequent years of education for black students who use a
voucher to switch from public to private school.'"*
—William Safire[186]

One of the main pillars of the conservative stance on education
is support for vouchers. Vouchers are cash awards of varied but
limited amounts that are given to a family to send their children
to private school if they wish—and if they can afford to make up
the difference between the voucher and private school tuition.
The idea behind vouchers is to give parents more choices and
improve education by forcing public and private schools to com-
pete for students.

For years, Republicans have been touting the need for vouchers, especially in poor urban areas. William Safire quoted from a
study performed at Harvard that looked at three small voucher
experiments in three different cities. Safire extolled the report,
which states that vouchers help African-Americans improve their
test scores, creating a "stunning reversal of their fortunes."[187]

The only problem with Safire's position is that subsequent
examinations of the data from that study show that vouchers
had little effect on students, regardless of race. Safire's own *New
York Times* revisited his assertions three years later:

Then, three weeks later, Professor Peterson's partner in the
study, Mathematica, a Princeton-based research firm, issued a
sharp dissent. Mathematica's report emphasized that all the
gains in Professor Peterson's experiment, conducted in New
York City, had come in just one of the five grades studied, the

sixth, and that the rest of the black pupils, as well as Latinos and whites of all grades who used vouchers, had shown no gains. Since there was no logical explanation for this, Mathematica noted the chance of a statistical fluke. "Because gains are so concentrated in this single group, one needs to be very cautious," it said.

Several newspapers wrote about Mathematica's report, but, coming three weeks after the first round of articles, these did not have the same impact . . .

David Myers, the lead researcher for Mathematica, is hesitant to criticize Professor Peterson. ("I'm going to be purposely vague on that," he said in an interview.) But he did something much more decent and important. After many requests from skeptical academics, he agreed to make the entire database for the New York voucher study available to independent researchers.

A Princeton economist, Alan B. Krueger, took the offer, and after two years recently concluded that Professor Peterson had it all wrong—that not even the black students using vouchers had made any test gains. And Mr. Myers, Professor Peterson's former research partner, agrees, calling Professor Krueger's work "a fine interpretation of the results."

What makes this a cautionary tale for political leaders seeking to draft public policy from supposedly scientific research is the mundane nature of the apparent miscalculations. Professor Krueger concluded that the original study had failed to count 292 black students whose test scores should have been included. And once they are added—making the sample larger and statistically more reliable—vouchers appear to have made no difference for any group.[188]

A more recent study by the Rand Group states that there *might* be some benefit for African-Americans through vouchers, but that hasn't been confirmed. And their study shows no net benefit for any other race from vouchers:

Academic Achievement

• Small-scale, experimental privately funded voucher programs targeted to low-income students suggest a possible (but as yet uncertain) modest achievement benefit for African-American students after one to two years in vouchers schools (as compared with local public schools).

• For children of other racial/ethnic groups, attendance at voucher schools has not provided consistent evidence of either benefit or harm in academic achievement.[189]

Researchers at Stanford University and the University of California at Berkley illustrated other problems with vouchers: They drain essential funds from public schools, and they do not provide enough of a subsidy for poor students to attend good private schools—meaning the children who most need improved educational opportunities are unable to benefit from vouchers:

California stands to lose $2.6 billion annually—and gain little academically—if voters pass the school voucher measure on the state ballot in November, a team of nonpartisan researchers is warning today.

Proposition 38 is intended to give fed-up public school parents a $4,000 voucher toward private or religious school tuition, courtesy of the California taxpayer.

The trouble is, it is unlikely that enough students could leave the public school system in order for the state to break even on the cost of the voucher program, say the researchers from Policy Analysis for California Education, a group of the University of California at Berkeley and Stanford University . . .

Their 15-page analysis slams the measure on several other fronts . . .

Low-income children who use vouchers could still not afford to attend elite schools of proven quality, where tuitions can cost well above $10,000 . . .

"This [measure] does not expand choice to more families," said [report co-author Luis] Huerta. "It's essentially tax relief for the well-off."[190]

If vouchers don't expand educational choice for poor children, and are simply tax relief for the well-off, it's hard to see why conservatives would support them.

ABANDONING "NO CHILD LEFT BEHIND"

"With passage of the No Child Left Behind Act in 2001, Bush neutralized the education issue, long a Democratic talking point."
—Fred Barnes[191]

Bush's first major initiative upon assuming office in 2001 was the No Child Left Behind Act, which he promised would cure the nation's educational ills. Bush proposed national standards, determined through testing, with assistance provided to those schools that couldn't make the grade. Eventually, parents would be provided with the opportunity to move their children out of "failing schools" if those schools didn't progress.

No Child Left Behind was initially viewed as an opportunity for liberals and conservatives to work together to improve education. Senator Ted Kennedy and Representative George Miller, two progressive leaders who have made education a priority during their time in Washington, worked with the president on the legislation in order to shape it into an acceptable form. The agreement between conservatives and liberals, Republicans and Democrats, was considered at the time to be evidence of President Bush's willingness to reach across the aisle to get things done.

Then came the double-cross. Having established a perception of bipartisanship on this crucial issue, the Bush administration abandoned No Child Left Behind.

While Barnes might believe that the passage of the bill is enough to "neutralize" education as a political issue in America, No Child Left Behind depends on significant and consistent funding. Not only did a national testing system need to be developed, but school aid needed to be reallocated and new schools needed to be built to move students out of substandard buildings. While the Bush administration continues to trumpet its education reform bill as a tremendous accomplishment, *it has yet to propose a budget that actually provides the funds authorized by the bill.*

Funding for reading, writing, and math programs for eco-nomically disadvantaged children (ESEA Title I programs) and special education for children with disabilities (IDEA) have been short-changed. In his most recent budget proposal, Bush asked for only 65 percent of the authorized funding for Title I programs and 50 percent of the authorized funding for IDEA.[192]

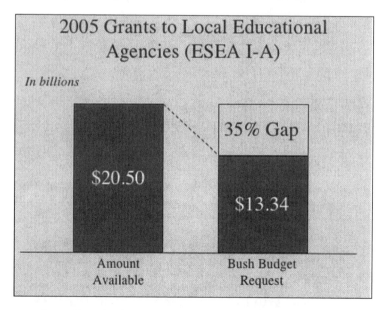

Source: Data taken from National Education Association, President's Budget Request For Fiscal Year 2005, Federal Education-Related Programs

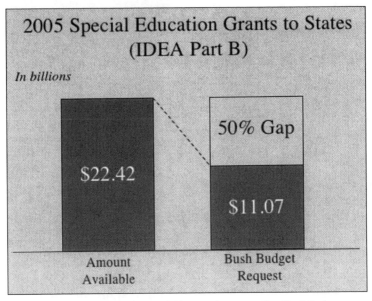

Source: Data taken from National Education Association, President's Budget
Request For Fiscal Year 2005, Federal Education-Related Programs

If conservatives really want to help improve education, they
could start by fully funding their own initiatives, instead of giving massive tax breaks to the wealthiest Americans.

THE PROVEN TRACK RECORD OF
PROGRESSIVE EDUCATION POLICY

*"The amazing thing is that Democrats and liberals had control of the edu-
cation system for 60 of the last 66 years. And they failed miserably at it."*
—Conservative commentator James Golden[193]

"The liberals are keeping kids in inner cities in these failing institutions."
—Sean Hannity[194]

Unfortunately for Golden and Hannity, in September 1993 the
Census published a document examining the educational
attainment of American citizens from 1940 to 1990. Not only

does the study report that "the proportion of Americans between the ages of 5 and 24 going to school has grown from 58 percent in 1940 to 70 percent in 1990," but also that we are "going to school earlier and staying in school longer."[195]

The report goes on to note:

Educational attainment levels for all person 25 years old and over have increased over the last 50 years. During the period from 1940 to 1990, the proportion of the population completing high school rose substantially.

Three-quarters of the adult population had completed at least a high school diploma in 1990 compared with about 25 percent in 1940, 41 percent in 1960, and 67 percent in 1980.

One-fifth of the adult population had completed a bachelor's degree or more in 1990 compared with about 5 percent in 1940, 8 percent in 1960, and 16 percent in 1980.[196]

Far from failure, the report paints a picture of consistent improvement in American education.

During the Clinton era, that progress was impeded by congressional resistance. Over the course of his administration, President Clinton consistently proposed increasing funding for education, but conservatives in Congress fought him at every turn.

Conservative pundit Bill O'Reilly has on at least three occasions aggressively argued that President Clinton failed to provide support for African-Americans to finish high school:

- *"Well, I look at eight years . . . of Clinton-Gore and I see a worse black student dropout rate in 2000 than in '92."*[197]

- *"Clinton didn't help blacks. He didn't help them. The black high school dropout rate in 2000 was higher than it was in 1992. All right?"*[198]

- *"See, look, I looked at the black high school dropout rates in '92 when Clinton took office, and then in 2000 when he left."*

> *That's eight years of—and African-Americans loved Bill Clinton.*
> *It's pretty much the same. Didn't improve in eight years.*[199]

O'Reilly is flat-out wrong. Despite opposition from conservatives in Congress, during the Clinton administration, the percentage of young African-Americans who had completed high school increased from 67.7 percent in 1992 to 78.9 percent in 2000. For young Hispanics, the increase was from 52.6 percent in 1992 to 57.0 percent in 2000.[200]

Table 8.—Years of school completed by persons age 25 and over and 25 to 29, by race/ethnicity and sex: 1910 to 2001

| | Percent, by years of school completed | | | | | | | | | | | |
| | Total | | | White, non-Hispanic [1] | | | Black, non-Hispanic [1] | | | Hispanic | | |
Age and year	Less than 5 years of elementary school	High school completion or higher [2]	4 or more years of college [3]	Less than 5 years of elementary school	High school completion or higher [2]	4 or more years of college [3]	Less than 5 years of elementary school	High school completion or higher [2]	4 or more years of college [3]	Less than 5 years of elementary school	High school completion or higher [3]	4 or more years of college [3]
1	2	3	4	5	6	7	8	9	10	11	12	13
	Males and females											
25 and over												
1910 [4]	23.8	13.5	2.7	—	—	—	—	—	—	—	—	—
1920 [4]	22.0	16.4	3.3	—	—	—	—	—	—	—	—	—
1930 [4]	17.5	19.1	3.9	—	—	—	—	—	—	—	—	—
April 1940	13.7	24.5	4.6	10.9	26.1	4.9	41.8	7.7	1.3	—	—	—
April 1950	11.1	34.3	6.2	8.9	36.4	6.6	32.6	13.7	2.2	—	—	—
April 1960	8.3	41.1	7.7	6.7	43.2	8.1	23.5	21.7	3.5	—	—	—
March 1970	5.3	55.2	11.0	4.2	57.4	11.6	14.7	36.1	6.1	—	—	—
March 1980	3.4	68.6	17.0	1.9	71.9	18.4	9.1	51.4	7.9	15.8	44.5	7.6
March 1985	2.7	73.9	19.4	1.4	77.5	20.8	6.1	59.9	11.1	13.5	47.9	8.5
March 1990	2.5	77.6	21.3	1.1	81.4	23.1	5.1	66.2	11.3	12.3	50.8	9.2
March 1992	2.1	79.4	21.4	0.9	83.4	23.2	3.9	67.7	11.9	11.8	52.6	9.3
March 1993	2.1	80.2	21.9	0.8	84.1	23.8	3.7	70.5	12.2	11.8	53.1	9.0
March 1994	1.9	80.9	22.2	0.8	84.9	24.3	2.7	73.0	12.9	10.8	53.3	9.1
March 1995	1.9	81.7	23.0	0.7	85.9	23.4	2.5	73.8	13.3	10.6	53.4	9.3
March 1996	1.8	81.7	23.6	0.6	86.0	25.9	2.2	74.6	13.8	10.4	53.1	9.3
March 1997	1.7	82.1	23.9	0.6	86.3	26.2	2.0	75.3	13.3	9.4	54.7	10.3
March 1998	1.7	82.8	24.4	0.6	87.1	26.6	1.7	76.4	14.8	9.3	55.5	11.0
March 1999	1.6	83.4	25.2	0.6	87.7	27.7	1.8	77.4	15.5	9.0	56.1	10.9
March 2000	1.6	84.1	25.6	0.5	88.4	28.1	1.6	78.9	16.6	8.7	57.0	10.6
March 2001	1.6	84.3	26.1	0.5	88.7	28.6	1.3	79.5	16.1	9.3	56.5	11.2

Rounds to zero.
—Not available.
[1] Includes persons of Hispanic origin for years prior to 1980.
[2] Data for years prior to 1993 include all persons with at least 4 years of high school.
[3] Data for 1993 and later years are for persons with a bachelor's or higher degree.
[4] Estimates based on Bureau of the Census retrojection of 1940 Census data on education by age.

NOTE: Total includes other racial/ethnic groups not shown separately.

SOURCE: U.S. Department of Commerce, Bureau of the Census, U.S. Census of Population, 1960, Volume 1, part 1; *Current Population Reports*, Series P–20 and un-published data; and 1960 Census Monograph, "Education of the American Population," by John K. Folger and Charles B. Nam. (This table was prepared September 2002.)

Throughout the Clinton administration, an increasing percentage of African-American students went on to college. In 1992, 48.2 percent of African-American high school graduates enrolled in college, while in 2000, 54.9 percent of African-American high school graduates enrolled in college. Young African-Americans were also more likely to have completed college during the Clinton administration. The percentage of young African-Americans who completed college rose from 11.3 percent to 16.6 percent; college completion increased from 9.2 percent to 10.6 percent for young Hispanics over the same period.[201]

Clinton's success in providing access to public education for minority students was matched by the success of the public education system in improving math and science education during Clinton's terms.

Between 1990 and 2000, during the Clinton administration, the percentage of public high school students taking advanced science and math courses increased significantly. More students are taking statistics, calculus, chemistry, biology, and physics than ever before.[202]

Table 141.—Percent of public high school graduates taking selected mathematics and science courses in high school, by sex and race/ethnicity: 1982 to 2000

						2000							
Courses (Carnegie credits)	1982	1987	1990	1994	1998	Total	Sex		Race/ethnicity				
							Male	Female	White, non-Hispanic	Black, non-Hispanic	Hispanic	Asian/Pacific Islander	American Indian/Alaska Native
1	2	3	4	5	6	7	8	9	10	11	12	13	14
Mathematics [1]													
Any mathematics (1.0)	98.5	99.0	99.9	99.8	99.8	99.8 (0.04)	99.8 (0.08)	99.9 (0.04)	99.8 (0.06)	99.8 (0.09)	99.8 (0.07)	100.0 (0.02)	100.0 #
Algebra I (1.0) [3]	55.2	58.8	63.7	65.8	62.8	61.7 (1.66)	60.0 (1.62)	63.4 (1.82)	60.5 (1.95)	66.5 (3.25)	69.5 (2.14)	48.8 (2.47)	65.2 (5.43)
Geometry (1.0)	47.1	58.6	63.2	70.0	75.1	78.3 (1.09)	74.9 (1.33)	81.4 (1.02)	79.2 (1.23)	77.9 (1.95)	72.8 (3.23)	80.6 (2.16)	65.0 (6.18)
Algebra II (0.5) [3]	38.9	49.0	52.8	61.1	61.7	67.8 (1.43)	64.8 (1.45)	70.5 (1.68)	68.9 (1.51)	64.8 (2.30)	59.8 (5.17)	80.4 (1.92)	60.3 (5.51)
Trigonometry (0.5)	8.1	11.5	9.6	11.7	8.9	7.5 (1.31)	7.3 (1.30)	7.7 (1.37)	8.5 (1.62)	4.1 (1.02)	2.9 (0.77)	14.5 (5.33)	4.3 (2.07)
Analysis/pre-calculus (0.5)	6.2	12.8	13.3	17.3	23.1	26.7 (1.40)	25.4 (1.39)	27.9 (1.61)	28.2 (1.74)	16.2 (1.53)	19.3 (2.97)	48.8 (2.68)	12.6 (2.80)
Statistics/probability (0.5)	1.0	1.1	1.0	2.0	3.7	5.7 (0.86)	5.8 (0.97)	5.6 (0.86)	6.1 (1.00)	3.8 (1.25)	2.3 (0.53)	11.5 (2.45)	2.1 (1.10)
Calculus (1.0)	5.0	6.1	6.5	9.3	11.0	11.6 (0.73)	12.2 (0.79)	11.1 (0.77)	12.5 (0.77)	4.7 (0.55)	5.6 (0.87)	30.8 (5.07)	2.4 (0.90)
AP calculus (1.0)	1.6	3.4	4.1	7.0	6.7	7.9 (0.58)	8.5 (0.71)	7.3 (0.57)	8.4 (0.82)	2.6 (0.41)	3.6 (0.68)	24.0 (4.20)	1.7 (0.70)
Science													
Any science (1.0)	96.4	97.8	99.3	99.5	99.5	99.5 (0.11)	99.3 (0.17)	99.7 (0.08)	99.6 (0.13)	99.5 (0.16)	99.1 (0.34)	99.7 (0.18)	99.6 (0.33)
Biology (1.0)	77.4	86.0	91.0	93.2	92.7	91.2 (1.00)	89.0 (0.32)	93.3 (0.80)	91.8 (1.15)	92.3 (1.02)	89.7 (2.70)	88.3 (2.70)	88.4 (2.88)
AP/honors biology (1.0)	10.0	9.4	10.1	11.9	16.2	16.3 (1.46)	13.8 (1.41)	18.5 (1.63)	17.9 (1.78)	10.8 (1.39)	10.8 (1.36)	25.9 (4.17)	8.0 (3.06)
Chemistry (1.0)	32.1	44.2	48.9	55.8	60.4	62.0 (1.47)	58.0 (1.42)	65.7 (1.74)	63.0 (1.87)	59.9 (2.40)	52.4 (4.08)	75.4 (2.59)	43.6 (4.03)
AP/honors chemistry (1.0)	3.0	3.5	3.5	3.9	4.7	5.8 (0.85)	5.8 (0.91)	5.7 (0.83)	6.1 (1.19)	2.8 (0.46)	3.4 (1.28)	16.2 (1.44)	1.7 (1.20)
Physics (1.0)	15.0	20.0	21.6	24.5	28.8	31.4 (1.16)	34.2 (1.29)	29.0 (1.22)	32.4 (1.34)	25.2 (1.98)	23.2 (2.32)	54.0 (2.68)	17.5 (4.07)
AP/honors physics (1.0)	1.2	1.8	2.0	2.7	3.0	3.9 (0.61)	5.4 (0.94)	2.5 (0.38)	4.0 (0.78)	2.2 (0.78)	2.0 (0.70)	11.0 (1.91)	0.5 (0.37)
Engineering (1.0)	1.2	2.6	4.2	4.5	6.7	3.9 (0.91)	4.3 (1.04)	3.5 (0.85)	4.2 (1.14)	2.7 (0.78)	2.4 (0.85)	3.1 (0.95)	1.8 (1.36)
Astronomy (0.5)	1.2	1.0	1.2	1.7	1.9	2.8 (0.59)	3.0 (0.65)	2.6 (0.57)	2.8 (0.68)	1.8 (0.54)	3.7 (1.54)	2.0 (0.69)	3.8 (1.67)
Geology/earth science (0.5)	13.6	13.4	24.7	22.9	20.7	17.4 (1.86)	18.4 (1.98)	16.6 (1.82)	17.5 (2.34)	18.6 (2.59)	15.9 (1.88)	11.1 (1.50)	16.0 (3.06)
Biology and chemistry (2.0)	29.3	41.4	47.5	53.7	59.0	59.4 (1.49)	54.5 (1.49)	63.8 (1.74)	60.3 (1.72)	58.0 (2.31)	50.4 (4.27)	71.1 (2.67)	39.4 (3.61)
Biology, chemistry, and physics (3.0)	11.2	16.6	18.8	21.4	25.4	25.1 (1.09)	26.4 (1.23)	24.0 (1.13)	25.7 (1.20)	20.1 (1.75)	17.6 (2.20)	47.2 (2.53)	11.9 (3.29)

\# Rounds to 0.00.
[1] These data only report the percentage of students who earned credit in each mathematics course while in high school and do not count those students who took these courses prior to entering high school.
[2] Excludes prealgebra.
[3] Includes algebra/trigonometry and algebra/geometry.

NOTE: Data differ slightly from figures appearing in other NCES reports because of differences in taxonomies and course exclusion criteria.
SOURCE: U.S. Department of Education, National Center for Education Statistics, "High School and Beyond," First Followup survey; "1990 High School Transcript Study," and "High School Transcript Study;" various years. (This table was prepared November 2002.)

Better preparation in public high schools has helped these students go on to advanced study in science and engineering. Graduate enrollment in science and engineering increased 9.4 percent between 1990 and 2000.[203]

It's hard to explain the right's consistent attacks on education, from their attempt to eliminate the Department of Education to their insistence on the flawed premise of vouchers. Even the bipartisan hopes of the No Child Left Behind Act have been dashed by the Bush administration's refusal to seek appropriate funding. It is not clear why conservatives are so insistent on cutting funding for education. But it is clear that cutting funding is what they try to do. Right-wing pundits' claims that conservative education policies will help the poor and minorities can be seen as attempts to cover up the truth: that those policies really mean deep cuts.

ENVIRONMENTAL POLICY
Conservative Commentators Treat Science As Optional

"IT'S RIGHT WHEN IT HELPS US": THE CONSERVATIVE DISDAIN FOR SCIENCE

"These people are nuts, folks. They're absolute wackos. They're total wackos."
—Rush Limbaugh, speaking of environmentalists[204]

Since the early 1990s, conservatives have been relentless in their attempts to roll back years of progress protecting our air, water, and open spaces, saying that government "overregulation" was not supported by scientific fact.

Unfortunately for Rush, science is on the environmentalists' side.

One of the first bills to pass the Republican Congress was so-called "regulatory reform" in which, according to *Business Week*, "the GOP [called] for scientific risk-assessment studies on rules that cost as little as $1 million. They want independent peer-review panels to oversee the research, and they want companies to be given the right to sue and recoup legal costs if the studies aren't done right."[205] That's right: Conservatives, usually so quick to attack lawyers and lawsuits, actually wanted polluters to be able to sue scientists if they didn't like the studies exposing their pollution.

The *St. Louis Post-Dispatch* reported in early 1995:

Risk assessment, cost-benefit analysis, "sound science"—these are terms that will be heard often in Congress as the Contract with America proponents tackle regulatory relief.[206]

Given conservatives' trumpeting of "sound science" and the dismissive comments of Limbaugh and his conservative cohorts, the recent stinging rebuke the Union of Concerned Scientists administered to the Bush administration for its widespread and unprecedented "manipulation of the process through which science enters into its decisions" is of particular note. In February 2004, the UCS, a group of preeminent scientists including Nobel laureates, National Medal of Science recipients, former senior advisors to administrations of both parties, numerous members of the National Academy of Sciences, and other well-known researchers, released the following statement:

When scientific knowledge has been found to be in conflict with its political goals, the administration has often manipulated the process through which science enters into its decisions. This has been done by placing people who are professionally unqualified or who have clear conflicts of interest in official posts and on scientific advisory committees; by disbanding existing advisory committees; by censoring and suppressing reports by the government's own scientists; and by simply not seeking independent scientific advice. Other administrations have, on occasion, engaged in such practices, but not so systematically nor on so wide a front. Furthermore, in advocating policies that are not scientifically sound, the administration has sometimes misrepresented scientific knowledge and misled the public about the implications of its policies.[207]

Accompanying their statement was a report documenting the numerous examples in which the Bush administration has "undermined the quality and independence of the scientific advisory system" across a broad range of policy areas from agriculture to national defense, from preventing lead poisoning to protecting endangered species.[208]

The current administration's tendency to ignore whatever facts get in the way of their ideology has certainly played out in their positions on the environment.

"BUT IT'S COLD OUTSIDE!": THE FAILURE TO UNDERSTAND GLOBAL WARMING

"A sparrow does not a spring make, but in the Druid religion of environmentalism, every warm summer's breeze prompts apocalyptic demands for a ban on aerosol spray and paper bags. So where is global warming when we need it?"
—Ann Coulter[209]

"Time now for the Most Ridiculous Item of the Day. Our pals over at MoveOn.org, a left-wing website, brought Al Gore in to speak about global warming today here in New York City, where it is eight degrees. Ridiculous? Only if Al didn't bring his mittens."
—Bill O'Reilly[210]

Global warming is, without a doubt, the favorite straw man of conservative pundits trying to justify their polluter-friendly ways. Conservatives seem to hope that if they deny the existence of global climate change long enough, they will rid themselves of the burdensome responsibility to protect the planet for future generations.

Let's dispense with Coulter and O'Reilly's simplistic understanding of the issue first. Global warming does not mean that every day will be warmer than the next. To the contrary, warming produces extreme weather on *both* ends of the temperature spectrum. Journalist Ross Gelbspan, who has covered the climate change debate in his career and is the author of a book about both sides of the argument, wrote regarding the consequences of warming:

> Scientists say these consequences will include not only more extreme temperatures, with hotter heat and colder cold, but also more intense rain and snowstorms, extraordinarily destructive hurricanes, and protracted, crop-destroying droughts, particularly in the interior regions of continents.[211]

In short, we can dispense with the facile and wildly misinformed question of why, if global warming is real, last winter was so cold. Last winter was so cold because global warming is real.

No matter how often conservatives deny the existence of global climate change, the evidence continues to point to a dramatic change in our climate with dire consequences should the trend continue. The planet is getting warmer. Temperatures at the Earth's surface increased by an estimated 1ºF over the 20th century. The 1990s were the hottest decade of the entire century, perhaps even the millennium, and 1998, 2001, and 2002 were three of the hottest years ever recorded.[212]

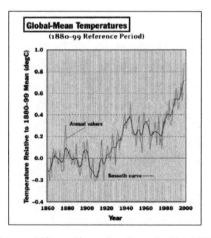

Source: The Science of Climate Change, Pew Center for Global Climate Change

Conservatives will say that 1ºF doesn't sound like much, but when Stephen Schneider, a climatologist at Stanford University, was asked whether a single degree of warming over the past century had a tangible impact, he replied:

> Melting glaciers are certainly tangible. Mountain glaciers have been reduced by about half. These things are receding. Sea levels are up 6 to 10 inches. And we've definitely seen an increase in heat waves and heat stroke deaths.[213]

Sean Hannity voiced another old conservative chestnut when, commenting on Al Gore's speech around the time of the release of the film *The Day After Tomorrow*, he asserted, "Even though scientists still can't agree on whether the global warming is scientific fact or fiction, the vanquished vice president, Al Gore, is using the film as an excuse to bash President Bush one more time."[214]

Hannity has it backwards. In fact, there is a remarkable degree of scientific consensus about global warming.

In January 2000, a blue-ribbon panel of climate scientists issued a report saying that global warming is "undoubtedly real." The panel, led by John Wallace at the University of Washington, reached agreement on the fact that global temperatures have risen more sharply in the past 20 years than at any time this century. Further, the National Academy of Science's National Research Council "took an unusually strong stand on the issue, and significantly undermined the principal argument used by scientists who dissent with the majority view . . . The panel of scientists said that contradictory evidence from satellite data, used by some scientists and political activists to dismiss reports of a warming planet, is irrelevant."[215] That didn't stop Hannity from calling Former Vice President Al Gore "an environmental extremist who uses hysteria to whip up a political viewpoint,"[216] when referring to Gore's speech about the consequences of global climate change.

When faced with such consensus, conservatives will sur-
render to their childish instinct to cry, "It's not our fault,"
claiming that current warming is natural, not driven by human
activities. James Glassman, relying on research by oil-funded
scientist Richard Lindzen, in an article titled "Bush Is Right on
Global Warming . . . *not that reporters would understand* . . ."
wrote:

> Such major climate swings occurred long before the industrial
> age. More important, the earth's cycles of warming and cooling
> predate human existence—not to mention sport-utility vehicles.
>
> But, in the view of the people we call "calamitologists," it is
> man—especially modern man—who despoils nature, stomping
> around in the Garden of Eden, killing rare species, dumping slop
> in the streams, and, in a final flourish, turning this beautiful
> green planet into an oven.[217]

Leaving aside Glassman's reliance on a source of dubious merit,
he's got his facts wrong. The Wallace Panel built on the compre-
hensive work of the United Nations–sponsored International
Government Panel on Climate Change, an effort of more than
2,500 scientists in 1995. Their report reached a near-unanimous
conclusion that global warming was at least partially a result of
human activity—primarily the burning of fossil fuels, which release
carbon dioxide, methane, and other gases into the atmosphere,
forming a global "blanket" that traps heat near the earth's surface.[218]

Given the unusually strong consensus in the scientific community that global warming is real and caused by human activity, it is surprising that there is any debate at all on the subject.
Part of the problem, unfortunately, is the way issues of global climate change are reported in the press. Gelbspan, a former editor and reporter for the *Boston Globe* and the *Philadelphia
Inquirer*, suggests:

One answer lies in the ethical standards of journalism. The professional canon of journalistic fairness requires reporters who write about a controversy to present competing points of view. When the issue is of a political or social nature, fairness—presenting the most compelling arguments of both sides with equal weight—is a fundamental check on biased reporting. But this canon causes problems when it is applied to issues of science. It seems to demand that journalists present competing points of view on a scientific question as though they had equal scientific weight, when actually they do not. The problem escalates because most journalists are not qualified to make judgments about issues such as standing, expertise, and integrity within the scientific community. As a result, ideology disguised as science can contaminate the debate.[219]

In spite of well-documented evidence arguing for action and consensus within the scientific community, one of Bush's first actions when he took office in 2001 was to withdraw from an international treaty on global climate change. By announcing that his administration would not seek to regulate carbon dioxide pollution from power plants—"a decision that amounted to effective abandonment of the Kyoto accord"[220]—Bush reversed a pledge he made while campaigning for office. As a candidate, the *New York Times* reported in 2000,

Mr. Bush has said . . . that he would support a requirement of some reductions in carbon dioxide emissions from power plants.[221]

"THIS IS SILLY": WHAT RIGHT-WING PUNDITS THINK ABOUT CLEAN AIR AND CLEAN WATER

"You know, if the arsenic levels stay the same and they didn't lower them to whatever extreme level they want, they're going to say the

Republicans want to poison the air, water and kill children. It's the same mantra. It's the same lies. It's the same misinformation."
—Sean Hannity[222]

"At almost exactly the moment that each environmental scare story exhausts its fundraising potential, along comes another, even more horrific than the last. It's safe to say that the excitement over Bush's revisions to the Clean Air Act won't be the last environmental blowup. It may, however, very well prove to be the silliest."
—David Frum[223]

Conservatives' constant denial of the scientific basis of environmental threats is only one tactic they employ to prevent environmental regulations. When they do propose environmental policy, it is almost always an attack on environmental protections in disguise.

Examining President Bush's record on our environment, it is hard to know where to start. While he couches his initiatives in the friendliest of terms—Healthy Forests, Clear Skies—in fact, his administration has been rolling back decades of progress cleaning up our air and water and protecting our open spaces.

Among his proposed policies: allowing increased arsenic levels in drinking water, making taxpayers (instead of the corporations who caused the mess) pay for toxic waste cleanup, clear-cutting our public forests, drilling for oil in wilderness areas and along our coasts, and letting old power plants continue to belch pollutants into the air instead of upgrading to cleaner technology. The list goes on and on.

Conservatives' dismissive attitudes about the risks pollution poses to the health of Americans is breathtaking. Consider Sean Hannity's contribution to this discussion of mercury pollution with Robert F. Kennedy, Jr.:

KENNEDY: It's coming from the power plants. We know a lot about mercury. One out of every six American women now has so much mercury in her womb that her children are at risk for a grim inventory of diseases, including autism, blindness, mental retardation, permanent cognitive impairment.

I have so much mercury in my body—I recently had it tested—that Dr. David Carpenter, who is the national authority on mercury, told me that if a woman of child-bearing years had the same levels that I did, that she, her—that she would have a child that would have permanent cognitive impairment . . .

Now listen, the Clinton administration, recognizing this problem, classified mercury as a hazardous pollutant under the Clean Air Act, which required those utilities to remove the mercury, 90 percent of it, within three and a half years. They can do it. It will cost less than one percent of the revenues of the plant.

PAT HALPIN [filling in for cohost Alan Colmes]: Now, Sean, you ought to be concerned about that.

HANNITY: This is silly.[224]

Almost immediately after taking office, Bush came under fire for attempting to roll back a Clinton administration regulation reducing the level of arsenic in drinking water—the first proposed change in arsenic regulation since the '40s. Newsday noted in an editorial:

Perhaps the new administration's most blatant dramatic environmental reversal was to rescind a Clinton holdover rule that would have reduced the allowable level of arsenic in drinking water by 80 percent, from 50 parts per billion to 10. Arsenic is not only a deadly poison in moderate doses but a carcinogen in minute ones; Clinton's environmental protection chief had recommended a drinking-water limit of 5 parts per billion.[225]

Although his conservative foot soldiers in the media, including Hannity, defended Bush's efforts to increase the amount of arsenic in our drinking water, public outcry forced President Bush to back down. But that didn't slow his efforts to weaken environmental protections. In April 2002, Bush released his deceptively named "Clear Skies" plan after rejecting the stronger protections included in an alternative proposal drawn up by his own Environmental Protection Agency that would have reduced air pollution further and faster.[226]

Bush's Clear Skies plan weakens the public health protections of the current Clean Air Act by delaying reductions in pollution emissions compared to enforcement of current law. For example, under current law, pollutants that cause soot and smog (sulfur dioxide and nitrogen oxides) must be cleaned up enough to ensure air quality meets public health standards by 2010. Under the Bush proposal, deadlines for meeting these public health standards would be delayed, allowing higher levels of soot and smog to continue until 2015 or later. The Clear Skies plan also does nothing to curb power plants' growing emissions of carbon dioxide, the main cause of global warming.[227]

Comparison of Bush administration air pollution plan with existing Clean Air Act programs:			
	Sulfur Dioxide	*Nitrogen Oxides*	*Mercury*
Increase allowed by Bush Plan over the current Clean Air Act	2010-2018: 2.5 million more tons per year	2010-2018: 850,000 more tons per year	2010-2018: 21 tons more per year
	after 2018: 1 million more tons per year	after 2018: 450,000 more tons per year	after 2018: 10 tons more per year
Percent Increase allowed by Bush Plan over existing Clean Air Act programs	2010-2018: 225% as much	2010-2018: 168% as much	2010-2018: 520% as much
	after 2018: 150% as much	after 2018: 136% as much	after 2018: 300% as much
Delay allowed by Bush Plan over Clean Air Act existing programs	Up to 6 year delay	Up to 8 year delay	Up to 10 year delay

Source: *Natural Resources Defense Council, citing EPA figures*

Bush's plan has been roundly criticized and for now remains blocked by Independent Senator Jim Jeffords, Democrats, and moderate Republicans in the Senate. In April 2002, the *New York Times* reported:

> A detailed bill sponsored by Senator James Jeffords of Vermont would regulate carbon dioxide as well as the other major pollutants. This bill is the only one with any traction in the Senate. Clear Skies, by contrast, is just a set of distant goals. As long as it remains so, it is hard to take Mr. Bush seriously.[228]

Such progressive efforts are absolutely crucial in preventing conservatives' unprincipled attacks on the environment.

Responsible members of both parties have historically come together to preserve our environment and natural resources, and have done the hard work of reconciling science with politics and policy. In response, conservative pundits call them "wackos" and "Druids." The dismissive "this is silly" that Sean Hannity offered when faced with the sobering impact of mercury levels is far too typical of conservatives' willingness to ignore science when it doesn't support their ideology.

"39 MILLION GREEDY GEEZERS"
What the Right-Wing Media Really
Thinks of America's Seniors

> *"There are . . . 39 million greedy geezers collecting Social Security.*
> *The greatest generation rewarded itself with a pretty big meal."*
> —Ann Coulter[229]

At first blush, the public conservative position on America's seniors seems cynically contradictory. On one hand, commentators like Coulter make defamatory statements about seniors. On the other, conservative politicians claim support for seniors and accuse progressives of trying to frighten America's older citizens.

It is in policy that this contradiction resolves itself. Conservative policies echo Coulter's "greedy geezers" shrillness and do little to help seniors. When it comes to America's seniors, clearly conservatives are interested in their votes, but not in their problems.

Ann Coulter is joined in the "greedy geezer" charge by Stephen Moore, president of the Club for Growth and a contributing editor of *National Review*. He has called U.S. citizens over the age of 65 "the most selfish group in America today" and a "dangerous" constituency:

> They have become the new welfare state, and given the size and
> political clout of this constituency, it's very dangerous. One of
> the biggest myths in politics today is this idea that grandparents

care about their grandkids. What they really care about is that that Social Security check and those Medicare payments are made on a timely basis.[230]

America's seniors aren't a "constituency" and they aren't "dangerous." To Stephen Moore and Ann Coulter they may be "greedy geezers" who don't care about their grandchildren. But to the rest of us, they're parents and grandparents, many of whom, despite what Moore says, played a crucial role in raising their children's children. They deserve better than denunciations from right-wing pundits whose goal is to generate support for policies against seniors' interests.

SENIORS' FIXED INCOME REALITY

Contrary to Coulter and Moore's right-wing rants about "greedy" seniors, most Americans over the age of 65 live on fixed incomes and worry about making ends meet. According to a May 2004 Gallup poll, "Retirement is one of Americans' biggest financial challenges, with half the population either very or moderately worried about not having enough money in retirement." The same poll found that "55% of current retirees . . . say Social Security is a major source of retirement income for them today."[231]

In 2002, the Employee Benefit Research Institute underscored senior reliance on Social Security, noting, "44% of retirees say Social Security was their primary source of income this year, up from 38% in 2000." [232]

In addition, the percentage of older Americans filing for bankruptcy is on the rise:

They are the fastest-growing group in bankruptcy. About 82,000 Americans 65 or older filed for bankruptcy in 2001, up 244% from 1991, according to the Consumer Bankruptcy Project, a study done at Harvard.[233]

So much for the right-wing media myth of greed and undue affluence among seniors.

RIGHT-WING PUNDITS ATTACK PROGRESSIVES WHEN BUSH BREAKS SOCIAL SECURITY PLEDGE

In a cynical attempt to capitalize on the financial difficulties of seniors, conservative Sean Hannity suggests that President Bush offers a useful policy:

> President Bush is investing hundreds of billions of dollars toward strengthening Medicare over the next decade, above and beyond the already planned annual increases. He proposes fully protecting the Social Security benefits of current and imminent retirees while giving young people the choice to invest a small percentage of their payroll taxes into their own personal retire- ment account if they so choose.[234]

What Hannity doesn't mention is that Bush has not kept his campaign promises to seniors.

As a presidential candidate in 2000, George W. Bush talked a good game for seniors, calling Social Security "the single most successful program in government history."[235] At the 2000 Republican convention, Bush categorically pledged to fight on the same side as older Americans: "To seniors in this country: You earned your benefits, you made your plans, and President George W. Bush will keep the promise of Social Security. No changes, no reductions, no way."[236]

But in August 2001—only seven months after taking office— President Bush went back on his word, as reported by USA Today:

> The White House is backing away from its pledge to protect every cent of Social Security reserves in the face of a report today that the government is tapping Social Security taxes for other programs.[237]

Not surprisingly, the all-spin response of right-wing media pundits was to attack progressives as demagogues, rather than to highlight the president's reversal. Sean Hannity, for example, ignored President Bush's broken promise: "One of the things that drives me crazy about the Democratic Party is I feel that they lie. I think they purposely try and scare old people during the election."[238]

Somehow, in Sean Hannity's head, *Bush's* broken promise was a reason to attack *Democrats* for "lying."

Hannity's rhetoric nicely matched that of conservative elected officials. Congressman Tom Davis, chairman of the National Republican Congressional Committee at the time, complained, "We have said for months that national Democrats are engaged in a cynical and deceptive campaign to scare seniors on the issue of Social Security."[239]

U.S. News & World Report contributing editor Steve Roberts (among many, many others) fell for the spin, announcing on CNN:

> The Democratic policy seems to consist of largely saying, "I told you so," which they have a right to say, but that's not a policy. And the fact is, they're left with two other things. One is rooting for the economy to slow down in order to justify their arguments, which is not a good position to be in. And the other is to demagogue Social Security.[240]

IF PRIVATIZATION IS THE ANSWER, WE'RE ASKING THE WRONG QUESTION

"Thirty-five million Americans bound together by a common love of airline discounts and automobile discounts . . . They're selfish, greedy. They don't care about their grandchildren a whit."
—Alan Simpson[241]

The importance of Social Security to most seniors' well-being is difficult to overstate. As the National Committee to Preserve Social Security and Medicare emphasizes, Social Security is a crucial building block of retirement:

> Social Security is the cornerstone of retirement: From the program's beginning, it was intended to be a base of protection, supplemented by private pensions and savings, not an individual's sole source of retirement income. Today, nine out of ten people over age 65 receive Social Security benefits. Two out of every three Social Security beneficiaries receive over half of their income from Social Security, and it's the only source of income for nearly one in five seniors. Without Social Security, most older Americans would live in poverty.[242]

Further, "Social Security has not contributed one cent to the federal deficit. It is about $150 billion in surplus this year and will continue to run a surplus through 2018." Indeed, "According to the Center on Budget and Policy Priorities, the 75-year cost of the administration's enacted and proposed tax cuts is three times the cost of permanently filling the 75-year gap in Social Security funding."[243]

We know from Bush's flip-flop (and defense of same by right-wing pundits) that conservatives don't actually want to protect every cent of Social Security. What *do* they want to do with this crucial program that doesn't impact our national debt? They want to gamble Social Security funds in the stock market, putting retirement funds at risk—but providing a huge windfall for Wall Street investment firms. (The securities and investment industry happens to be one of the top donors to both George W. Bush and the Republican Party.)[244]

Conservatives like Townhall.com columnist David Limbaugh position this as a question of ownership:

Despite what they said then, the Democrats are morbidly fearful of any restructuring of Social Security involving private accounts. How can you explain their opposition to privatization when it will almost surely result in greater returns and thus enhance the system's solvency? Easy.

Under current law, workers and retirees have no legal ownership over their benefits; merely a political promise that can be revoked at any time. Partial privatization will invest workers with a degree of ownership and security. Hallelujah! But Democrats aren't joining in the chorus, because worker ownership means less government dependency and a threat to their cinch lock on the minority vote.[245]

What arguments like Limbaugh's ignore is the "security" part of Social Security. If conservatives succeeded in privatizing Social Security, Americans would need to dedicate a significant portion of their attention to managing their Social Security funds in the stock market. And while America's stock market is certainly filled with opportunities, there are no guarantees that our seniors would be protected. Indeed, as the National Committee to Preserve Social Security and Medicare points out:

Privatization turns Social Security from a guarantee into a gamble: Privatization places the entire risk of having a decent retirement income on the individual, instead of spreading risk throughout the workforce as Social Security currently does. Even relatively safe investments, such as state or local government bonds, are subject to potentially significant risk for an individual investor. Stock markets can go both up and down, and relying on private accounts means people will have to carefully time their retirement to avoid the bad years. Unfortunately, many people learned this lesson the hard way during the most recent market downturn. From 1999 to 2003, the value of

401(k) accounts owned by people near retirement dropped by an average of 25%. This caused millions to keep working years longer than they had originally planned to make up the difference. Placing Social Security savings into these same Wall Street accounts magnifies the risk many times over.[246]

The same group makes the point another way:

... Privatization will dismantle Social Security. The transition to private accounts will be costly, requiring trillions of dollars from general revenues. There will be no guarantees as to the future earnings on these private accounts. They can fail just as easily as they succeed—mirroring the unpredictable nature of the investment markets.[247]

Leaving our seniors beholden to the whims of the market is not the only problem with privatization. The costs of privatization mean that "taxes would have to be increased significantly, massive new government debt incurred, or guaranteed benefits dramatically scaled back,"[248] in order to balance the cost, as even President Bush's own commission admits:

President Bush's Social Security Commission set out three options today for allowing workers to establish individual investment accounts and acknowledged that the proposals would have to be accompanied by benefit cuts or other painful steps if the retirement system was to avert a long-term financial crisis ... "No matter how you approach it, individual accounts make it more difficult to meet the challenges Social Security faces in the future," said Representative Robert T. Matsui, a California Democrat who is a senior member of the Ways and Means Committee. "To pay for privatization, the commission is now proposing serious benefit cuts."[249]

RIGHT-WING COMMENTATORS TRASH MEDICARE

During the mid-1990s—the halcyon days of the ill-fated Gingrich Revolution—right-wing commentators and Republican elected officials showed their true hostility to seniors and Medicare.

Rush Limbaugh declared in July 1995 that Medicare had "contributed greatly to the demise of our country" and complained that it wasn't possible to chew out Lyndon Johnson for the program's alleged "mismanagement." Limbaugh also dismissed progressive defenders of Medicare as "relics" of a bygone era:

> We don't have the money for this anymore. We are broke. Now the guy who came up with this, LBJ, is dead. Where do we go to complain . . . Who do we complain to about the mismanagement of this program? The guy who started it. If we're customers and you guys are the business, who do we complain to? Nobody having to do with this is still around and you relics want it to survive as it was.[250]

Limbaugh also defended the Republican plan to "reduce the Medicare increase"[251] and protested, "Where is it written that Medicare recipients should receive a gift of 5 1/2 percent every year when salaried workers aren't getting that in their wage increases every year. Where is it written?"[252]

Official right-wing hostility to Medicare in 1995 was expressed by then–House Speaker Newt Gingrich, who explained the GOP's strategy: "We didn't get rid of it in round one because we don't think that that's politically smart and we don't think that's the right way to go through a transition. But we believe it's going to wither on the vine because we think people are voluntarily going to leave it."[253]

Conservative pundit Linda Chavez defended the Gingrich

assault on Medicare in 1995, calmly (if inaccurately) noting, "All of the polls show that exactly what the Republicans are doing is very popular."[254]

Fast-forward eight years, and right-wing hostility to Medicare remains routinely popular—at least among Republican politicians and conservative commentators:

- *"I believe the standard benefit, the traditional Medicare program, has to be phased out."* —Senator Rick Santorum (R-PA)[255]

- *"Medicare is a disaster . . . We have to understand that Medicare, in order to work properly, is going to have to be overhauled from top to bottom as quickly as possible . . . [L]et's create a whole new system."* —Senator Bob Bennett (R-UT)[256]

- *"Some of our friends on the other side of the aisle are saying that if this bill becomes law, it will be the end of Medicare as we know it. Our answer to that is, we certainly hope so. Why should seniors be the last group that pays retail prices for drugs? Old-fashioned Medicare is not very good."* —Representative Bill Thomas (R-CA)[257]

- *"The Medicare delivery system is antiquated, fragmented, and overly bureaucratic."* —Senate Majority Leader Bill Frist (R-TN)[258]

In 2003, conservative commentator Charles Krauthammer lauded President Bush for going along with Congress in its hostility toward the Medicare program, noting, "I want to say what's impressive about the Medicare is that he's going after very big issues. He's taking very high risks. He's touching the third rail—on Medicare . . ."[259]

Give Krauthammer credit. He's consistent. Consistently wrong, but consistent nonetheless. In 1999, he implied that Medicare was unnecessary and criticized President Clinton for proposing a prescription drug benefit:

Clinton, relentlessly waving the Social Security/Medicare banner, is feeding the piggishness. And even adding to it by proposing a new prescription drug benefit at a time when two-thirds of seniors—who, incidentally, have a lower poverty rate than the rest of the population—already have prescription drug coverage.[260]

Four years later, in 2003, Tucker Carlson joined the chorus of conservative commentators who view seniors as "piggish geezers" looking for unnecessary handouts:

> If you look at the surveys of people who actually need money for prescription drugs, there's not some huge percentage of Americans who can't pay the prescription drug bills.[261]

In their attacks on seniors, Carlson and Krauthammer ignored the soaring costs of health care and likelihood of dis-continued supplemental drug coverage for fixed-income seniors. As USA Today noted in 2002:

> Out-of-pocket health care expenses for seniors increased nearly 50% from 1999 to 2001, according to a report by the Commonwealth Fund. The costs are likely to go up as more employers eliminate retiree health benefits, which typically pro-vide supplemental drug coverage.[262]

Right-wing media propaganda characterizing America's seniors as greedy also conveniently overlooks the fact that "nearly half of the elderly people who end up in bankruptcy say that they filed because of a medical reason," as noted by USA Today in 2002.[263]

Conservative commentators and their GOP allies do, how-ever, gloat at the political box into which (they believe) they have placed their Democratic adversaries. Laura Ingraham—columnist, TV commentator, and former law clerk to Supreme Court Justice Clarence Thomas—is combative in making that point:

I think the Democrats have really relied on scaring Grandma that she's going to be forced to eat Alpo for the next couple of years if George Bush or any Republican gets into office. They're going to get those prescription drug cards right away. That's something tangible they can hold in their hands. I think that, in and of itself, is a powerful statement.[264]

A CONFUSING, EXPENSIVE, AND FAILED NEW PRESCRIPTION DRUG PROGRAM

"The president has been very consistent in that he promised to provide a prescription drug benefit to seniors, and he delivered on that promise."
—Conservative pundit Kellyanne Conway[265]

"I mean, there was one hugely important measure that passed [the Senate], that was the prescription drug benefit that may be the most important domestic measure passed in, in decades . . ."
—Fred Barnes[266]

Contrary to the cheerleading by right-wing pundits, the National Committee to Preserve Social Security and Medicare tells us that the new prescription drug program signed by President Bush doesn't do nearly enough to help seniors on fixed incomes:

In one of its greatest failings, the legislation is woefully lacking in any meaningful containment of the skyrocketing price of either prescription drugs or health care . . . The law also fails to make it any easier to reimport drugs from Canada or other countries, despite the fact that many of those drugs were originally manufactured in the United States and are significantly cheaper abroad.[267]

In addition, inflation and the lack of price containment could quickly eliminate the program's few advantages:

Families USA found prices of the 30 most popular drugs used by seniors increased at four times the rate of general inflation during 2003, and AARP found a 28% increase in a broader list of drugs from 2000 to 2003 . . . [T]he drug benefit that looks meager today will only become worse with time. According to Medicare's own Trustees, within a few short years seniors will need to have over $8,580 in covered drug costs to trigger the catastrophic coverage.[268]

In his analysis of the program, Congressman Henry Waxman (D-CA) concluded that the program had resulted in "chaos" among seniors who must choose among dozens of discount card programs. "No matter how much Republicans torture the data, it is evident that the cards won't give seniors the savings they need," Waxman said in a statement. "After seeing what the new cards offer, the overwhelming response is confusion and dismay."[269]

Luisa Kaufman-Phelan, president of the Arizona Alliance, warned, "This bill has a lot of little loopholes and they're all starting to surface right now . . . Confusing is not the word. It is so convoluted."[270]

It's no wonder that Senator Jay Rockefeller (D-WV) concluded, "It's a failed bill and now it seems to be a much more, expensive, failed bill."[271]

Conservative pundits often accuse liberals of trying to scare seniors. Their accusation would make more sense if there wasn't plenty to be frightened of. From their disdain for Medicare to their plan to privatize Social Security, conservatives seem set on dismantling the support structure for America's seniors. Though conservative politicians talk a good game in order to seek seniors' votes, the "greedy geezers" snarling of right-wing pundits exposes the true feelings (or lack thereof) of the right.

NOT WHAT YOU HEAR ON TV
The Comparative Record on Crime and Public Safety

"Look at the two main things in the 1990s that helped urban blacks. One was welfare reform, which reduced the child poverty rate. The other was get-tough-on-crime policies, which led to a drastic decline in murders and other crimes in the inner city. Who advocated those policies? Who were the main advocates? Conservative Republicans . . . It was the higher imprisonment rate since the 1970s that steadily put more and more people in jail through get-tough-on-crime conservative policies, and steadily that wore down the crime problem."
—Rich Lowry[272]

Conservative ideologues like *National Review* editor Rich Lowry constantly claim that conservative "tough-on-crime" policies work, and that liberals are "soft on crime." So when President Clinton presided over eight consecutive years of declining crime rates, due in part to his crime bill, the Brady Bill, the assault weapons ban, and the COPS program, what do these conservative pundits say? They say it was *conservative* policies that led to the reduction in crime.

Why, then, with conservatives in control of every branch of government, have crime rates been on the rise? According to Eric Lichtblau in the *New York Times*:

Murder rates are edging up around the country. In the shadow of the White House, the capital has suffered a rash of gang violence and car thefts, with five people shot in one attack last week. And police chiefs nationwide complain that federal officials are cutting back the money they need to protect their cities.[273]

Despite the "tough-on-crime" reputation of President Bush, "Murders were up 1.3 percent nationwide. In the Northeast, murders increased 5.1 percent, and small towns saw a spike of 15.7 percent."[274]

In addition, a separate Justice Department review this year found that "42% of the 2,182 cities that responded to the 2002 National Youth Gang Survey reported that gang activity was 'getting worse,' up from 27% the previous year. In the same survey, 87% of U.S. cities with populations of at least 100,000 reported problems with gangs."[275]

USA Today recently reported that, nationwide, gang-related homicides jumped by 50 percent from 1999 to 2002. And in 2002, the most recent year analyzed, 1,034 of the 16,204 homicides across the nation were linked to gangs—the most since 1995, when there were 1,237 gang-related slayings.[276]

The International Brotherhood of Police Officers (IBPO)—which endorsed George W. Bush in 2000—has concluded that Bush "turn[ed] his back on America's police officers as president. He has cut the COPS program in every one of his budgets and threatened the overtime pay of officers across the country. He has also made it harder for police to do their jobs on the frontlines by not giving states and local communities the resources they need to fight the war on terror."[277]

Since becoming president, George W. Bush has cut federal grants to pay for local police personnel, equipment, and training. He's also cut millions of dollars from the Community Oriented Policing Services (COPS).[278] After pledging to expand anti-drug programs,[279] the president has moved to cut funding from the Office of National Drug Control Policy.[280] At the same time, murder rates are inching up—after years of decline. Police chiefs across the country complain that the Bush administration won't provide the funding to fight crime in local communities.[281]

By any objective standard, the case should be closed: *progressives* are tough on crime; *conservatives* are soft on crime.

Unfortunately, objective standards aren't the ones used by right-wing pundits or conservative commentators.

THE CLINTON RECORD: RIGHT-WING FEAR MONGERING IGNORES DROP IN CRIME

Crime used to be a much easier issue for right-wing pundits. Back in the 1990s, all you had to do was attack President Clinton for pervasive crime and appointing liberal judges—even if it wasn't true.

The charge against Clinton was that he had some sort of secret agenda to appoint liberal judges who, if the pundits were to be believed, would then release violent criminals and sex offenders, thus doing irreparable harm to America's law-and-order culture.

According to conservative commentator Thomas Sowell, "Judges that Clinton puts on the federal benches all across the country will be able to turn criminals loose for decades into the 21st century."[282] Recognizing that Clinton was running for re-election in 1996 as a crime fighter, Sowell warned, "Once re-elected, he will of course drop the pretense and go back to the usual liberal big-spending, growing government, racial quotas, and soft-on-crime judicial appointees." Sowell ominously predicted that it would take "decades, if not generations, to recover from the effects of a second Clinton administration."[283]

Richard Lessner of the *Union Leader* in New Hampshire warned his newspaper's readers in 1996 of "all those liberal judges . . . who keep letting all those thugs, drug dealers, murderers and rapists off easy."[284]

Likewise, the *Tampa Tribune* exhorted voters "to look beyond the rhetoric" and consider Clinton's appointment of "permissive justices who attempt to inject social activism into the law [and] are eager to unshackle criminals from the law, while quick to handcuff police in their efforts to protect the public."[285]

Conservative Cal Thomas approvingly repeated Bob Dole's allegation that Clinton was soft on crime, had "an elitist view of America," and "appointed liberal judges who have waged war with our values."[286]

They were all wrong. Crime dropped during the Clinton years, as tough *and smart* (conservatives are pretty good at the first part, but haven't mastered the second yet) progressive policies proved effective.

In 1996, even while the right-wing pundits and Republican politicians were attacking Clinton as weak on crime, the FBI was reporting reductions in robbery (seven percent), rape (six percent), and aggravated assault (three percent).[287]

That year, crime fell in every category and in every region of the country, dropping most sharply—four percent—in the Northeast. The Midwest saw a two percent decline; the South and West recorded one percent reductions.[288]

According to the FBI:

• New York, Chicago, Los Angeles, and other cities with more than one million people reported the largest decline—six percent.

• Smaller cities of 500,000 or more saw an increase of one percent, while rural counties reported a three percent increase in crime.

• Total property crimes dropped one percent, auto theft was down six percent, and burglary fell five percent.

• Violent crime dropped four percent last year as overall serious offenses reported to police declined for the fourth straight year.

• Murder declined most dramatically, falling eight percent to about 21,400 murders for 1995, down from a peak of about 24,700 murders in 1991.[289]

The dramatic drop in crime—according to Alfred Blumstein, criminology professor at Carnegie Mellon University and a researcher for the Department of Justice—was attributable in part to the Clinton administration's push to put 100,000 more police on the streets through the Community Oriented Policing Services (COPS) program and aggressive programs to get guns out of juvenile hands.[290]

Conservative ideologues never gave President Clinton credit for the unprecedented crime reduction during his term of office. For example, years after Clinton left office, columnist Mona Charen was still churlish about the COPS program:

> Did crime decline? Well, as a matter of fact it did. Did the program contribute to this drop in the crime rate? Very doubtful. The Office of Community Oriented Policing Services performed a self-audit and concluded that the program was working out exactly as planned. The Heritage Foundation, the Office of Management and Budget, and the Justice Department have concluded otherwise.[291]

Former Reagan aide and current right-wing pamphleteer Dinesh D'Souza wouldn't give Clinton credit for peace, prosperity, or falling crime rates, rationalizing:

> Our current peace and prosperity are very much a legacy of the Reagan era. Ironically, Bill Clinton has been surfing on a wave of public goodwill that was generated by Reagan's achievements.[292]

The most strenuous contortion of right-wing logic, however, comes from the *Wall Street Journal*, which in 2003 gave Attorney General John Ashcroft—not Bill Clinton—credit for the decline in gun violence during the 1990s:

The results are a vindication for Mr. Ashcroft, who has been vilified for being soft on gun violence because he continues to defend the constitutional rights of law-abiding gun owners. In reality, gun violence has declined from 12% of violent crime in 1993 to 9% in the most recent Justice statistics. Any gun control advocates out there care to apologize?[293]

Anyone at the *Wall Street Journal* care to remember that John Ashcroft wasn't attorney general during seven of the ten years in which gun violence was declining? Anyone at the *Journal* want to explain why gun control advocates would *apologize* for a decade that saw the creation of two significant gun control laws—the Brady Bill, requiring a waiting period for handgun purchases, and the assault weapons ban—accompanied by a reduction in gun violence?

"TOUGH ON CRIME"?: BUSH HAS *CUT* ANTI-CRIME PROGRAMS

When Bush was beginning his presidential campaign in 1999, the respected *National Journal* observed, "No one would ever accuse Bush of being soft on crime . . . The tough-on-crime approach appears to have paid dividends: Texas' crime rate is at its lowest point in the past 20 years."[294]

The assumption that Bush would be "tough on crime" was common in the media, but Bush has been anything but tough. Instead, he and his administration have consistently tried to cut funding for successful progressive anti-crime initiatives, and are poised to let the assault weapons ban, which helped keep deadly, military-style weapons off America's streets, expire.

In mid-2002, Attorney General Ashcroft seemed to praise— without actually crediting—the success of President Clinton's anti-crime COPS program:

Since law enforcement agencies began partnering with citizens through community policing, we've seen significant drops in crime rates.[295]

Ashcroft even said that the COPS nationwide network of Regional Community Policing Institutes had been "successful in reducing crime, in preventing crime, reducing the incidence of breaches of personal and community security all across the United States."[296]

Ashcroft's public praise of COPS was consistent with a 2000 study by Urban Institute that found COPS to have had a "broad national impact" on police work, including "now-familiar cop bike patrols and an increased emphasis on prevention through closer contact with citizens."[297]

But Ashcroft's public talk was inconsistent with the actual policy of the Bush administration, which has cut COPS funding.

In 2001, President Bush announced that he planned to reduce the COPS budget from $1 billion to $855 million. Administration officials said there was no proof that the program had reduced crime.[298]

In 2003, the Bush administration again announced cuts to COPS because the program's "impact on crime is inconclusive."[299]

The Bush cuts to law enforcement caused concern at the National League of Cities, which warned that the cuts would lead to police layoffs and a reduction of local law enforcement grants by 40 percent.[300]

Sadly, that isn't the only way the Bush administration has cut effective anti-crime programs and made us less safe at home—with the full-throated support of conservatives in the media.

In 1997, midway through the Clinton administration, the *Wall Street Journal* attacked the "baby boom" morals of the president and first lady, suggesting that they were somehow personally responsible for "whacked out" drug offenders:

Could all of you 30-something professionals in places like Manhattan, L.A. and San Francisco find something to do other than suck cocaine up your noses? Could you upper-middle-class suburban parents find the courage to just once deprive your obviously whacked-out children of something that is destroying their lives? And could the Baby Boom U.S. President and his wife possibly find time routinely in their schedules to personally put some moral leadership behind the idea that using this stuff is bad?[301]

Three years later, during the 2000 presidential campaign, then-Governor George W. Bush continued the attack, accusing the Clinton administration of fighting illicit drugs "without urgency, without energy, and without success." He also attacked the Clinton administration for supposedly cutting the staff of the White House drug office from 146 to 25 people—"about half the size of the White House public relations operation." Promising to do better, Bush proposed $2.7 billion in new grants in the next five years to combat narcotics and provide drug treatment.[302]

Bush was, at the very least, mistaken in his assertions, according to the Office of National Drug Control Policy. Personnel cuts at the White House Drug Office had been reversed to the point that the office actually had 154 staff members. Teenage drug use had not just leveled off, it had declined 21 percent from 1997 through the end of 1999.[303]

Not only was Bush wrong about Clinton's anti-drug efforts, he has failed to follow through on his own promises to do better. In May 2004, Bush proposed cutting the budget of the High Intensity Drug Trafficking Areas (HIDTA) program, which combats drug trafficking, by $18 million, or 8 percent.[304]

In 2001, President Bush promised to prioritize "the problem of domestic violence in our communities every day of the year."[305] Again in 2003, he pledged, "My administration is fighting domestic violence and strengthening services for victims and their dependents."[306]

But in 2004, the president moved to cut or freeze funding for domestic violence programs. According to United States Senator Patty Murray, "The President's budget cuts . . . a Justice Department rape prevention program by $29 million. It freezes funding for the Domestic Violence Hotline. And it freezes funding for Grants for Battered Women Shelters at precisely the time when we need increases because evidence shows that domestic violence increases during tough economic times."[307]

HOMELAND SECURITY AS PHOTO OP, NOT FUNDING PRIORITY

Bush's cuts to domestic violence programs likely have the support of conservative pundits like Ann Coulter, who has referred to the Violence Against Women Act as "feminist lunacy."[308]

But why do conservative pundits support the Bush administration's deep cuts to programs local law enforcement officials depend upon to keep us safe and secure?

Homeland Security Director Tom Ridge and the Bush administration talk about security and law enforcement a lot. The president himself "stands proud—shoulder-to-shoulder with heroes of the NYPD—in photo-ops and campaign ads."[309] But the word is starting to get out that Bush and his administration officials "are taking credit for spreading largess through programs that President Bush tried to eliminate or to cut sharply"[310]—or worse, "decimating" federal programs on which local police agencies depend to supplement limited local resources.[311]

According to the National League of Cities and published news reports, the Bush administration is making or proposing cuts to grant programs to finance local police personnel, equipment, and training,[312] and programs that fund the First Responder Initiative, as well as housing and community development funding.[313]

The Bush cuts come at a time when the federal government

is asking local law enforcement to do more, not less, to protect ports, airports, businesses, and public infrastructure.[314] In addition, local law enforcement agencies have either laid off uniformed officers or failed to fill the slots vacated by retirees.[315]

According to the *New York Times*:

- Cleveland has laid off 250 police officers (15 percent of its total force).

- Pittsburgh has lost one-quarter of its police officers over the last three years.

- The Los Angeles County Sheriff's Department has let go 1,200 deputies in the last two years, leading it to close several jails and release a number of inmates early.

- Houston has laid off 190 jail guards.

- Cleveland has assigned detectives to patrol duties, eliminating gang units and auto theft squads.[316]

Conservative columnist Mona Charen, for one, has defended the Bush administration and sarcastically dismissed concerns that cities and states are not receiving adequate resources to protect their citizens:

> If the Democrats want to argue that the best response to 9-11 is better port inspection and radiation detectors at airports, that's fine. In his speech Sunday night, the President reiterated what he has said many times since 9-11. We are fighting with our soldiers and Marines there so that we will not have to fight with our police, firemen and doctors here.[317]

But it's not just Democrats who argue that the homeland is less secure when our hometowns lose police officers and civil defense capabilities. Even Republican governors, according to the *New York Times*, "sounded worried about whether [National Guard] deployments would leave them vulnerable in emergencies."[318]

The *New York Times* also noted that governors in all regions of the country have "complained to senior Pentagon officials that they were facing severe manpower shortages" because National Guard units have been deployed to Afghanistan and Iraq:[319]

- In Washington State, 62 percent of the state's 87,000 Army National Guard soldiers are deployed, including the majority of the guard's best-trained firefighters.[320]

- In Oregon, troop deployments have left that state's National Guard with half the usual number of firefighters because about 400 of them were overseas.[321]

- In Alaska, 15 percent of its National Guard members are stationed overseas.[322]

- In Arizona, more than 130 prison guards are serving overseas, short-staffing already crowded prisons.[323]

- In Tennessee, rural sheriff's and police departments have been depleted by the guard call-up.[324]

Like Charen, Sean Hannity doesn't see a problem with Bush's cuts to essential programs. In his book *Let Freedom Ring*, Hannity praises President Bush for his "crisp moral clarity" and for being "straightforward, honest, passionate" in his defense of America.[325] Hannity also gushes that with Bush as president, "Our military and intelligence services will now receive the kind of respect and financial support they need in order to protect us."[326]

But Hannity—like most pundits on the right—has been conspicuously silent about President Bush's failure to provide the necessary respect and support for our local law enforcement agencies and civil defense needs.

After four years of "tough-on-crime" George W. Bush, according to the *New York Times*, "There's a real frustration within the law enforcement community" that crime issues are not commanding more attention in the presidential and down-ballot campaigns.[327]

Crime, public safety, and homeland security, like fiscal responsibility, are areas in which the popular perception of liberals and conservatives is contradicted by the public record. While it is often assumed that conservatives are tougher on crime and stronger defenders of the homeland, the current administration's cuts to the COPS program and decision to turn a deaf ear to the cries of cities and states for more help on homeland security run counter to that misperception. And while conservatives imply that liberals' concern for individual rights makes them soft on crime and public safety, the record shows that progressives have a strong record of putting police on the street and decreasing crime.

NO SENSE OF SHAME
Conservative Pundits' Destructive Rhetoric About Values

"My friends, this election is about much more than who gets what. It is about who we are. It is about what we believe. It is about what we stand for as Americans. There is a religious war going on in our country for the soul of America. It is a cultural war, as critical to the kind of nation we will one day be as was the Cold War itself. And in that struggle for the soul of America, Clinton & Clinton are on the other side, and George Bush is on our side. And so, we have to come home, and stand beside him."
—Patrick Buchanan[328]

"Although 1864 and 2004 are vastly different times, there is a similarity. Now as then, America is at war, albeit this time with an external enemy; and now as then, some Democrats do not seem to be on the side of their own country."
—James Taranto[329]

Pat Buchanan's speech at the 1992 Republican convention is generally thought of as a blunder that helped cost George H.W. Bush his presidency. But the last 12 years have shown that Buchanan's speech wasn't an anomaly, and it wasn't a case of a fringe character giving the right a bad name. Rather, it was a clear and accurate illustration of the leadership of the modern conservative movement: angry, divisive, and, above all, intolerant. Those who side with Buchanan believe that progressive policies and politicians have led this country astray because they don't believe in "family values."

While conservatives give significant lip service to the right of an individual to make any choices they like, much of their public rhetoric focuses on forcing others to comply with conservative ideas of morality. Too often, conservatives cry loudly that they need not comply with anyone else's idea of what's right ("It's a free country!"), while at the same time condemning non-conservatives and seeking to marginalize, or even ban, their viewpoints.

Unfortunately, conservatives cravenly employ the rhetoric of values in order to win support from those who are hurt the most by conservative policies, as Thomas Frank points out in his book, *What's the Matter with Kansas?*:

> The Movement's basic premise is that culture outweighs economics as a matter of public concern—that *Values Matter Most*, as one backlash title has it. On those grounds it rallies citizens who would once have been reliable partisans of the New Deal to the standard of conservatism. Old-fashioned values may count when conservatives appear on the stump, but once conservatives are in office the only old-fashioned situation they care to revive is an economic regimen of low wages and lax regulations. Over the last three decades they have smashed the welfare state, reduced the tax burden on corporations and the wealthy, and generally facilitated the country's return to a nineteenth-century pattern of wealth distribution. This is the primary contradiction of the backlash: it is a working-class movement that has done incalculable, historic harm to working-class people.[330]

George W. Bush has put a softer face on the same old divisive conservative attacks, by calling himself a "compassionate conservative" while pursuing the same policies and taking the same "us-vs.-them" approach Buchanan used years before. While trying to appear "compassionate" (or "kinder, gentler," as his father put it), Bush's constant suggestions that people who love freedom agree with him (implying that people who disagree with him must hate freedom) are just as divisive as anything Buchanan ever said. Where Buchanan advertised his hate by speaking of a "religious war" for the "soul of America," Bush relies on the subtle but insidious suggestion that to disagree with him is to disagree with America, with freedom itself.

Some of Bush's ideological cohorts in the media dispense with the subtlety and simply accuse progressives of being anti-American. Conservative James Taranto of the *Wall Street Journal*, for example, has written:

> If you listen to prominent Democrats like Ted Kennedy, Robert Byrd and Al Gore, it's hard to avoid the conclusion that they'd rather see America lose the war than the president win re-election. It's bad enough that one party is willing to engage in what as a practical matter amounts to anti-American propaganda.[331]

While conservatives use values language as a blunt object in an attempt to bludgeon their opponents into submission, they also use it as a shield to protect themselves from charges that they've done little to help those most in need. When progressives dare to question Bush administration policies, conservative pundits denounce them as full of "hate," as FOX News contributor Morton Kondracke did when discussing the Democratic Convention:

> You know, there was so much Bush hatred among the Democratic activists here at the convention that if they start throwing them red meat, God knows what might happen.[332]

FOX anchor John Gibson likewise dismissed Democrats as driven by hate:

It's true that hating George W. Bush has been the fuel that has driven the Democratic machine for months, if not years, but it's going underground for now . . . [T]he Dems can try to hide the fact that what motivates Democrats this year is how much they hate George W. Bush.[333]

But despite conservatives' values-laden rhetoric, and angry denunciation of progressives, the left has proven itself to be far more family-friendly than the right. During the Clinton years, progressive leaders pushed forward pro-family agendas and values, with statistically demonstrable success. It seems that when it comes to values, the only difference between liberal thinkers and conservative commentators is that progressives seem far more interested in providing tangible support to families, while conservatives have used word and deed to split our nation apart.

CLINTON-ERA PROGRESS ON FAMILY ISSUES

Fewer Abortions

"Finally, all the candidates are willing to sell out any of these other issues in service of the secret burning desire of all Democrats: abortion on demand. If they could just figure out a way to abort babies using solar power, that's all we'd ever hear about."
—Ann Coulter[334]

Ann Coulter's outrageous claim that Democrats' sole desire is for "abortion on demand" is unfortunately typical of the kind of hyperbole that conservatives bring to this complex and emotional discussion. While the right focuses on demagoguery, progressives have simultaneously worked to defend the rights of American women and to advance policies that reduce the root causes of abortion: teenage pregnancy, poor education, and inadequate health care. From the conservative attacks on liberal "abortion on demand" policies, one would assume that the number of abortions would have skyrocketed during the presidency of the only Democrat in the past 24 years.

To the contrary, the abortion rate declined under Bill Clinton. When he took office in 1992, he inherited from the first President Bush an abortion rate of 25.7 per 1,000 women. By 1999, the last year for which the Census offers figures, that number had declined to 21.4 abortions per 1,000 women. The overall number of abortions declined from 1,529,000 in 1992 to 1,315,000 in 1999.

Both the abortion rate and the total number of abortions were higher under adamantly pro-life, but decidedly not progressive President Ronald Reagan. When Reagan left office in 1988, the number of abortions totaled 1,591,000 and the abortion rate was 27.3 per 1,000 women.[335]

Fewer Teenage Pregnancies

"You see, there are two areas of study in the schools, upper and lower. The lower studies have to do with the left's preoccupation on all things below the belt. That would be lessons on human sexuality, gender bending, sex, abortion, sexual orientation, condoms, oh, and did I mention sex? Basically, members of the left are intellectuals at the crotch level."

—Michael Savage[336]

While Savage and his brethren concentrate on smearing those who don't share their extremist views, the drastic reduction in the number and rate of abortions under Bill Clinton illustrates that the progressive approach of providing true family-planning education and support to American citizens is more effective than conservative "family values" rhetoric. The point is further illustrated by the decreased number of teenage pregnancies during Clinton's presidency.

In 1990, 521,826 teenage girls gave birth. By the time Clinton left office in 2000, the number of teenage moms declined by nearly 53,000 to 468,990. Further, from 1994 to 2000, the number of teenage births declined every year.

While there are many possible reasons for the drop in teenage birth rates, one likely cause is that the number of women using contraceptives rose from 1982 to 1995, according to the Centers for Disease Control, National Center for Health Care Statistics.

From 1982 to 1995, the number of women using birth control increased from approximately 54 million to more than 60 million.[337] Of all the different methods of birth control, the largest increase came from the number of women using condoms. From 1982 to 1995, the percentage of women using condoms as contraceptives went from 12 percent to 20.4 percent.

The sharpest increase in condom usage occurred amongst women under the age of 25. Women ages 15 through 19 increased their usage of condoms from 20.8 percent in 1982 to 36.7 percent in 1995, while women ages 20 through 25 increased their usage from 10.7 percent in 1982 to 26.4 percent over the same period.[338] As teenage pregnancies decreased at the same time condom use among teenage women increased, it is likely that there is a causal link between them. Despite conservative claims that education about condoms violates "family values," it seems that encouraging condom use amongst young people has a significant impact in preventing teenage pregnancy. The only question remaining is whether "family values" rhetoric, especially that as ugly as Savage's, is more important than tangible results.

Lower Divorce Rate

"The whole notion of two-parent family, with a dad and mom who are married and fully committed to each other for the long haul—

regardless of what struggles come their way—is another of the ideals
that's under siege. We live in an age characterized by the maxim, 'If
it feels good do it—regardless of the consequences.'"
—Sean Hannity[339]

Conservatives have also blamed liberals and their 1960s lifestyle for the breakdown of the traditional family. The argument is that liberal contempt for the 1950s *Leave it to Beaver* family structure has contributed to the moral breakdown of society.

Of course, Republican respect for family structure depends on who the family is. Conservatives have launched vicious attacks on high-profile Democratic wives, from Hillary Clinton to Linda Daschle and now Teresa Heinz (whom Chris Wallace of FOX News compared to the wife of a dictator by saying of her speech at the Democratic Convention, "[B]y the end, I half expected her to break out into 'Don't Cry for Me, Argentina'").[340]

Regardless of their hypocrisy, the numbers don't bear out Republican attacks on Democrats. For instance, under Bill Clinton, the divorce rate in this country declined. When he took office in 1992, the annual divorce rate was 4.8 per 1,000 people. By 1997, that number tumbled to 4.3 per 1,000—a 10 percent decrease in the divorce rate in just five years. (Data for years since 1997 is incomplete, but based on the data that is available, the divorce rate continued to decline through 2001.)

Again, Clinton bested Reagan on a so-called "family values" statistic. During the first five years of the Reagan administration (from 1981-1985), the annual divorce rate was more than 5 per 1,000 people. The *lowest* rate of divorce during the Reagan Presidency was 4.8; the *highest* rate under Clinton was 4.7.[341]

CONSERVATIVE OPPOSITION TO
FAMILY-FRIENDLY LEGISLATION

RAY FLYNN: What—what am I? I mean, I'm pro-life. I'm pro-family. You know, I'm against the death penalty. I'm for the working class, needy, poor. Does that make me a conservative?

SEAN HANNITY: Well, yeah.[342]

In July 2004, John Kerry said, "It is time for those who talk about family values to start valuing families."[343] It was his way of pointing out that Republican talk about family values is just that—talk. Republicans often oppose legislation designed to help working families.

The clearest example of conservative opposition to family-friendly policies was the "Family and Medical Leave Act." The bill allowed family members to get time off from work to care for a child or a sick relative. Quite simply, it allowed people to keep their jobs if they had to miss work in order to take care of their family.

"Family values" conservatives fought the bill tooth and nail. Republican Tom DeLay opposed the Act, calling it "unwieldy" and claiming Congress has "no business, no right, and no ability to legislate how the American family should apportion the burden of caring for its own." It seems that while conservatives are eager to legislate on the definition of "family" itself, they see no contradiction in arguing that the government has "no business, no right, and no ability" to help families care for themselves, and are worried instead about the impact on American businesses.[344]

George H.W. Bush, the man who brought us the family values theme, twice vetoed the Family and Medical Leave Act, criticizing it in much the same way DeLay had, as an unnecessary federal mandate and burden on business.[345]

Bush's veto of such a family-friendly bill drew heavy condemnation, even from pro-business publications such as *Business Week*, which noted that Bush's veto belied his "family values" campaign strategy:

> The GOP's campaign emphasis on family values would be a lot more believable if President Bush ignored ideology and signed this modest family-leave legislation.[346]

President Clinton made the Family and Medical Leave Act the first piece of legislation he signed upon taking office in 1993. In 1996, Clinton said of the law, "All the bill says is if you work in a business with 50 or more employees and your spouse is about to have a baby, or you are, or your mama or your daddy's real sick, or your baby's real sick, you can take just a little time off from work without losing your job. Now, you tell me, is that anti-business? If it's anti-business, how did this economy produce 10.5 million new jobs? That's more jobs, more job growth, faster rate, than any Republican administration in 70 years."[347]

Indeed, contrary to conservative assertions that the law would impose a crushing burden on business, the *New York Times* reported in 1998:

> Many employers have found that the law has not hurt productivity or profits, according to Donna Lenhoff, vice chairwoman of the Family Leave Commission, a bipartisan group set up by Congress to evaluate the law's effects.
>
> Indeed, a survey conducted for the commission in 1994 and 1995 found that of 1,206 employers questioned nationwide, more than three-quarters said the law was not difficult to administer or obey in most cases, Ms. Lenhoff said. She said 89 percent of employers reported little or no increase in administrative expenses because of the law.[348]

Progressives chose to help families; conservatives chose to pander to big business. The results have been clear: Family and Medical Leave has helped families, at little cost to business.

Conservative opposition to the Family and Medical Leave Act is only one of many family-friendly policies the right-wing has fought at every turn. Conservatives oppose minimum wage increases, education funding, improved and affordable access to health care. They oppose workplace safety rules, overtime pay, and meaningful prescription drug programs. They oppose limits on how much arsenic can be in our kids' drinking water, and they oppose school-lunch programs. They try to cut loan and grant programs that help middle-class and poor children attend college, and they want to divert Social Security funds into the stock market.

And Sean Hannity says conservatives are "pro-family" and "for the working class, needy, poor."

Incredible.

THIS IS DECENCY?: CONSERVATIVE COMMENTATORS' OUTRAGEOUS POSITIONS ON GAY MARRIAGE AND HUMAN RIGHTS

"When you hear the words 'Human Rights Commission,' you know what you're dealing with. Think of the worst people in America, they're the ones who go on to human rights commissions. They're neo-fascists in the guise of human rights activists. They wanna tell you what you can think, what you can't think. Who you can listen to, who you can read—they're stinkers. They're communist or Nazis or both . . . So they're attacking the San Francisco Police Officer's Association, because the San Francisco Police Officer's Association received free tickets to my event, Michael Savage Uncensored . . . Now I'm extremely popular, but the San Francisco Human Rights Commission thinks that their Nazi background gives them an opportunity to say that I'm a hateful person because they don't like what I

say about homosexuals . . . When you hear 'human rights,' think gays. When you hear 'human rights,' think only one thing: someone who wants to rape your son. And you'll get it just right. OK, you got it, right? When you hear 'human rights,' think only someone who wants to molest your son, and send you to jail if you defend him. Write that down, make a note of it."
—Michael Savage[349]

Discussing homosexuality with Michael Savage is no doubt like trying to discuss science with someone who believes the moon is made out of green cheese: Little progress is likely to be made, because he doesn't approach the topic from a rational perspective.

While Savage will likely never escape his sad little alternate universe of hate, it's worth pointing out, for the benefit of those who may have a more open mind, that Savage is completely wrong. Hard as it may be to believe that in 2004 we need to repeat the scientific opinion that there is no link between homosexuality and pedophilia or rape, here it is:

"It's important for people to know that being gay has nothing to do with pedophilia," said Dr. Larry Harmon, a Miami psychologist whose practice specializes in sexual orientation issues. "Being gay is a sexual orientation. Pedophilia is a psychological disorder."

Dr. Michael Rappaport, a Miami psychologist who is treating Levy in prison, said there is a major difference between homosexuality and pedophilia:

"Pedophiles want to have sex with little children. Homosexuals want to have sex with other men," he said.

"Pedophiles get insulted if you suggest they are gay."

Rappaport, a heterosexual doctor with many gay clients, says, "There is a prejudice that gay males are out there seducing straight boys. That pedophiles are gay men. That's so unfair to the gay community."

Gregory M. Herek, a psychology professor at University of California/Davis, said many pedophiles are neither homosexual nor heterosexual.

"They have no adult sexual attraction. It's clearer to refer to it as male-male or female-female sex," said Herek, who has extensively studied and written about sexual orientation issues, including child molestation.[350]

Attacks like Savage's have been too common as homosexuals attempt to win the right to marry, an issue that angers conservatives so much that they are willing to justify hate speech in their attacks on the supporters of the issue, as Pastor Paul Morton did on *Scarborough Country*:

Marriage in this nation is going the way of Sodom and Gomorrah was, totally against God, and, of course, it was destroyed because of low morals. We are talking about hate crimes now and calling it hate. Years ago we used to call it good morals, but now it's called hate. I think we have our agendas confused.[351]

In spite of the vitriol spewed by conservatives against allowing homosexuals to marry, it could be argued that gay marriage is actually a pro-family proposal. First, children raised by homosexual parents suffer no unusually ill effects:

One of the most commonly cited studies actually assessing the effect on children was published in 2001 by University of Southern California Professors Judith Stacey and Timothy Biblarz, who favor same-sex marriage but nonetheless set out to critique studies suggesting there were no differences between children raised in gay and straight families . . .

Stacey and Biblarz find that gay parenting "has no measurable effect on the quality of parent-child relationships or on children's mental health or social adjustment." This, as it happens, was also the determination of the American Psychological Association (APA) after an extensive 1995 review of the literature on gay families. Children raised by gay parents, the APA concluded, are not "disadvantaged in any significant respect relative to the children of heterosexual parents." The American Academy of Child and Adolescent Psychiatry echoed this finding in its 1999 statement opposing discrimination against gay parents. Ditto the American Academy of Pediatrics in a 2002 policy statement, saying children of gay parents have "the same advantages and the same expectations for health, adjustment, and development" as those of heterosexual parents. Indeed, not a single reputable study shows any harm whatsoever to children living in same-sex-headed households.[352]

Further, there are significant benefits to the couples allowed to marry:

[T]he research that is least disputed in the budding marriage movement is that married people are happier, healthier, wealthier, and in a better position to raise kids. They are less likely to commit suicide, to have fatal accidents, or to suffer from alcoholism and depression, and they earn more money and report better sex lives than singles. And, not only are married people happier individuals, they are more productive citizens. All the data, in other words, points toward extending the benefits of marriage to as many people as can fulfill its social function.[353]

Conservatives' hateful attacks don't end with gay marriage. Those questioning whether conservatives are willing to sacrifice human and civil rights to advance their agenda need to consider that Michael Savage won't vote for a Democrat because he's "not voting for a party of ethnic minorities and women and immigrants."[354]

Sean Hannity demonstrated an amazing callousness toward human rights during the trial of New York City police officers accused of abusing an immigrant. As documented by FAIR (Fairness and Accuracy in Reporting):

> When Haitian immigrant Abner Louima accused New York City police officers of sodomizing and badly injuring him with a wooden rod in 1997, Hannity used his WABC show for a vicious counter-offensive targeting the victim.
>
> The father of chief defendant Justin Volpe, an NYPD police officer, regularly appeared on the show during the 1999 trial. And Hannity and various guests repeated rumors that Louima's injuries resulted from a "gay sex act" and not from police brutality. Playing on the homosexual rumor and inconsistencies in Louima's story, Hannity and his producer sang a parody of Lionel Richie's song, "Three Times a Lady," changing the words to, "You're once, twice, three times a liar." Hannity stopped referring to the victim as "Lying Louima" only after Volpe confessed to sodomizing Louima with the help of another officer . . .[355]

Despite their horrifying dismissal of human rights, despite their callous rejection of family-friendly policies, conservatives continue to claim they hold the moral high ground and proclaim themselves the defenders of "family values."

Since we know they can't be talking about their policy positions, and we know they can't be talking about how they treat other people, conservatives must be talking about how they live their own lives when they claim the moral high ground.

Indeed, when confronted with the demonstrable success of progressives' family-friendly policies, conservatives often retreat to *ad hominem* attacks against President Clinton, Ted Kennedy, and others they like to demonize as morally bankrupt. But while prominent conservatives have criticized other people for not holding the right "values," many conservatives haven't been able to live up to their own rhetoric. Two wrongs don't make a right, and we don't intend to catalogue the personal peccadillos of those conservatives whose hypocritical public statements make such an exercise tempting. But conservatives' willingness to publicly condemn activities they are privately engaged in looks not just hypocritical, but dishonest, and demonstrates that, for all their use of the topic as a political tool, they assign very little worth to "family values"—except as a weapon with which to attack their opponents.

In that way, at least, conservative commentators like Rush Limbaugh, Sean Hannity, and Ann Coulter talk about "values" precisely as they talk about so many other things. Not as a serious topic worthy of serious discussion, but as a weapon. They approach "values" not as something real, with real meaning, but as something to be twisted, shaped, distorted, and lied about for whatever small advantage they can gain.

ACKNOWLEDGMENTS

Misstating the State of the Union was made possible by numerous people. *Media Matters Action Network's* Jamison Foser coordinated all the research, writing, and editing efforts. Brett DiResta, Mike Rice, Alexis Schuler, and Craig Varoga conducted the bulk of the research and did much of the writing. John Fishback generously provided essential last-minute writing and editing assistance. *Media Matters Action Network* President David Brock provided invaluable leadership throughout.

Source materials cited in the endnotes span a wide breadth of print and broadcast media sources as well as books, government reports, and scholarly studies too numerous to single out for specific acknowledgment.

The book also draws heavily—in content and in spirit—on research, writing, and editing previously done and posted at mediamatters.org. This book provides a small sample of the type of conservative misinformation that the smart, dedicated, and talented staff of *Media Matters for America* responds to day in and day out. Thanks to everyone at *Media Matters Action Network* and *Media Matters for America* for their ongoing hard work in exposing conservative misinformation in the media.

The idea of writing a book that would analyze both the success of recent progressive and conservative policy positions, and how those positions have been misreported and distorted by various media figures, belongs to Richard Foos, whose generous financial support brought the project into being.

We'd like to thank as well Johnny Temple and all the folks at Akashic Books for their hard work and efforts to produce the book on schedule, and in accord with their high standards; and Robert Greenwald for introducing us to Akashic Books.

Finally, we'd be remiss in failing to acknowledge our friends in the conservative media, whose low standards gave us a lot of material with which to work.

ENDNOTES

[1] Linda Chavez, "The Bush Economy?" Townhall.com, May 21, 2003
[2] *Associated Press*, July 11, 1983, no headline
[3] George Will, "This Week With George Stephanopoulos," ABC News Transcripts, June 13, 2004
[4] Editorial, "Gloom and Boom," *Wall Street Journal*, June 14, 2004
[5] FOX News Channel's *Hannity and Colmes*, March 16, 2004
[6] Ann Coulter, "Just Say Yes: It's the Clinton Economy!," anncoulter.com, October 16, 2003
[7] George Will, "This Week With George Stephanopoulos," ABC News Transcripts, June 13, 2004
[8] Hall, Robert, et al., "The Business Cycle Peak of March 2001," NBER website, November 26, 2001
[9] Sean Hannity website, www.hannity.com, August 3, 2004
[10] FOX News Channel's *Hannity and Colmes*, April 6, 2004
[11] FOX News Channel's *Hannity and Colmes*, March 26, 2004
[12] FOX News Channel's *Hannity and Colmes*, March 16, 2004
[13] FOX News Channel's *Hannity and Colmes*, March 3, 2004
[14] FOX News Channel's *Hannity and Colmes*, February 23, 2004
[15] FOX News Channel's *Hannity and Colmes*, November 6, 2002
[16] Editorial, "That '90s Show," *Wall Street Journal*, July 28, 2004
[17] Dana Milbank, "As 2004 Nears, Bush Pins Slump on Clinton," *Washington Post*, July 1, 2003
[18] George W. Bush, Radio Address, Transcript from Whitehouse.gov, December 1, 2001
[19] White House Press Releases, Remarks by the President at Republican Governors Association Fall Reception, September 20, 2002
[20] Dana Milbank, "As 2004 Nears, Bush Pins Slump on Clinton," *Washington Post*, Tuesday, July 1, 2003, P. A11
[21] Peter Huessy, Kerry's Deficit; Presidential Hopeful Lacks Fiscal Judgment," *Washington Times*, December 6, 2002
[22] Newt Gingrich, *Fox News Sunday*, August 1, 2004
[23] Donald Luskin, "Truth Matters," *National Review Online*, May 5, 2004
[24] Nell Henderson, "Recession Could Have Begun Early; Research Group Ponders Setting Start Date in Late 2000," *Washington Post*, January 23, 2004
[25] Dana Milbank, "Experts Date It to Bush; Bush Says It Was Clinton's," *Washington Post*, March 5, 2004
[26] Tucker Carlson, CNN's *Crossfire*, July 16, 2004
[27] "National Employment, Hours and Earnings," Bureau of Labor Statistics, 1994-2004, http://data.bls.gov/cgi-bin/surveymost
[28] Jonathan Fuerbringer, "Bush's Race Against Kerry (And Hoover)," *New York Times*, August 1, 2004
[29] David Wessel, "Bush, Kerry Are Both Right on the Economy," *Wall Street Journal*, July 1, 2004
[30] Jonathan Fuerbringer, "Bush's Race Against Kerry (And Hoover)," *New York Times*, August 1, 2004
[31] Brit Hume, FOX News Channel, *Special Report with Brit Hume*, May 20, 2004
[33] Jon E. Hilsenrath and Sholnn Freeman, "So Far, Economic Recovery Tilts To Highest-Income Americans," *Wall Street Journal*, July 20, 2004
[34] Jon E. Hilsenrath and Sholnn Freeman, "So Far, Economic Recovery Tilts To Highest-Income Americans," *Wall Street Journal*, July 20, 2004
[35] The average worker's purchasing power, CITE
[36] Stephen S. Roach, "More Jobs, Worse Work," *New York Times*, July 22, 2004
[37] Stephen S. Roach, "More Jobs, Worse Work," *New York Times*, July 22, 2004
[38] Stephen S. Roach, "More Jobs, Worse Work," *New York Times*, July 22, 2004
[39] Stephen S. Roach, "More Jobs, Worse Work," *New York Times*, July 22, 2004
[40] Bill O'Reilly, FOX Radio Network, *The Radio Factor*, June 11, 2004
[41] Editorial, "Two Americas? Yes. But look what divides them," *USA Today*, July 28, 2004
[42] Eduardo Porter, "Hourly Pay In U.S. Not Keeping Pace with Price Increases," *New York Times*, July 18, 2004
[43] Jay Hancock, "Once Again, It's a Bad Job Growth Economy," *Baltimore Sun*, July 18, 2004
[44] Stephen S. Roach, "More Jobs, Worse Work," *New York Times*, July 22, 2004
[45] Eduardo Porter, "Economy Slowed In 2nd Quarter, U.S. Report Says," *New York Times*, July 31, 2004
[46] Linda Chavez, CNBC's *Dennis Miller*, June 18, 2004

[47] Press Release, "Employment Up, Wages Flat, for Hispanic Workers," Grantee Press Releases: Pew Hispanic Center, June 16, 2004

[48] Vanessa Fuhrmans, "Fewer Workers Have Health Benefits," *Wall Street Journal*, August 3, 2004

[49] Bob Herbert, "An Emerging Catastrophe," *New York Times*, July 19, 2004

[50] Charles Babington, "South Dakota's Allure Tops Boston's," *Washington Post*, July 16, 2004

[51] Eduardo Porter, "Economy Slowed In 2nd Quarter, U.S. Report Says," *New York Times*, July 31, 2004

[52] Jon E. Hilsenrath and Sholnn Freeman, "So Far, Economic Recovery Tilts To Highest-Income Americans," *Wall Street Journal*, July 20, 2004

[53] Vanessa Fuhrmans, "Fewer Workers Have Health Benefits," *Wall Street Journal*, August 3, 2004

[54] Stephen S. Roach, "More Jobs, Worse Work," *New York Times*, July 22, 2004

[55] Rush Limbaugh, *The Rush Limbaugh Show*, April 29, 2004

[56] Edmund Andrews, "A Growing Force of Nonworkers," *New York Times*, July 18, 2004

[57] Edmund Andrews, "A Growing Force of Nonworkers," *New York Times*, July 18, 2004

[58] Edmund Andrews, "A Growing Force of Nonworkers," *New York Times*, July 18, 2004

[59] Rush Limbaugh, *See, I Told You So*, New York: Pocket Books, 1993, p. 297

[60] David E. Rosenbaum, "White House Says $445 Billion Deficit Forecast Isn't as Bad as It Looks," *New York Times*, July 31, 2004

[61] David E. Rosenbaum, "White House Says $445 Billion Deficit Forecast Isn't as Bad as It Looks," *New York Times*, July 31, 2004

[62] David E. Rosenbaum, "White House Says $445 Billion Deficit Forecast Isn't as Bad as It Looks," *New York Times*, July 31, 2004

[63] David E. Rosenbaum, "White House Says $445 Billion Deficit Forecast Isn't as Bad as It Looks," *New York Times*, July 31, 2004

[64] Fred Barnes, FOX News Channel's *FOX Special Report With Brit Hume*, May 19, 2004

[65] Leigh Strope, "New Manufacturing Czar Tapped; First Pick Withdrew Over Outsourcing Flap," *Associated Press*, April 8, 2004

[66] Press Release, "Press Briefing By N. Gregory Mankiw, Chairman of the Council of Economic Advisers, on the 2004 Economic Report of the President," Office of the Press Secretary, February 9, 2004

[67] Randy McSorley, "Bush Worked Overtime to Kill OT for Others," *Post-Crescent*, April 25, 2004

[68] "Bush Budget Cuts Funding for Job Training and Employment Services," Democratic Policy Committee, 2003

[69] Newt Gingrich, "Newt's Goals for America's Future," *Insight on the News*, March 16, 1998

[70] Rush Limbaugh, "The Deficit & National Debt," www.rushlimbaugh.com, March 12, 2004

[71] David Stockman, *The Triumph of Politics*. Quoted by Tom Raum, "Stockman Balmes President's 'Awesome Stubborness' for Growing Deficit," *Associated Press*, December 30, 1986

[72] Robert S. Boyd, "Huge Imprint on Nation, Relatively Little on Policy," *Miami Herald*, June 6, 2004

[73] Chris Edwards," Reagan's Small-Government Vision," *National Review Online*, June 9, 2004

[74] Jeff Jacoby, "Bring Back Reagan's RX," *Boston Globe*, July 25, 2002

[75] David Stockman, *The Triumph of Politics*. Quoted by Matthew Benjamin, "David Stockman," *U.S. News and World Report*, April 19, 2004

[76] Lou Cannon, "Actor, Governor, President, Icon," *Washington Post*, June 6, 2004

[77] Al Franken, *Rush Limbaugh is a Big Fat Idiot*, New York: Island Books, 1996, p. 145

[78] Donald Lambro, "GOP's Muted Budget Response . . . and Reflexes," *Washington Times*, February 17, 1997

[79] Emily Newman, "News in Brief: OMB Projects $331B FY '05 Deficit," *The Bond Buyer*, August 2, 2004

[80] Sean Hannity, FOX News Channel's *Hannity and Colmes*, March 10, 2004

[81] CNN, *In the Money*, March 6, 2004

[82] "The Budget and Economic Outlook: An Update," Congressional Budget Office, August 2001

[83] "Bush Still on Track to Borrow $10 Trillion by 2014", Citizens for Tax Justice, January 30, 2004 www.ctj.org/pdf/def0104.pdf

[84] Sean Hannity, *Let Freedom Ring*, New York: HarperCollins Publishers Inc., 2002, p. 215

[85] FOX News Channel's *Hannity and Colmes*, January 30, 2004

[86] George W. Bush, Northern Michigan University, Marquette, Michigan, Tuesday, July 13, 2004, http://www.georgewbush.com/News/Read.aspx?ID=2949

[87] FOX News Channel's *The O'Reilly Factor*, May 12, 2003

[88] Jeff Birnbaum, "Bush Continues to Ignore Veto Power," *Marketplace*, February 16, 2004

[89] *Associated Press*, "McCain Decries Spending," *New York Newsday*, December 1, 2003

[90] James Flanigan, "Why Dollar Worries May Be Just a Distortion," *Los Angeles Times*, July 18, 2004

[91] John Gibson, FOX News Channel's *Hannity and Colmes*, May 7, 2004

[92] James Traub, "The Things They Carry," *New York Times Magazine*, January 4, 2004

[93] "'We are all Americans,' proclaims France's *Le Monde* newspaper," Agence France Presse, September 12, 2001

[94] British Prime Minister Tony Blair, September 11, 2001, "America's Response to Terrorism: *Quotes*," The Brookings Institute, 2004, http://www.brookings.edu/dybdocroot/fp/projects/terrorism/quotes.htm

[95] French President Jacques Chirac, September 11, 2001, "America's Response to Terrorism: *Quotes*," The Brookings Institute, 2004, http://www.brookings.edu/dybdocroot/fp/projects/terrorism/quotes.htm

[96] German Chancellor Gerhard Schroeder, September 11, 2001, "America's Response to Terrorism: *Quotes*," The Brookings Institute, 2004, http://www.brookings.edu/dybdocroot/fp/projects/terrorism/quotes.htm

[97] Russian President Vladimir Putin, September 12, 2001, "America's Response to Terrorism: Quotes," The Brookings Institute, 2004. http://www.brookings.edu/dybdocroot/fp/projects/terrorism/quotes.htm

[98] George W. Bush, "Speech: President Says Saddam Hussein Must Leave Iraq Within 48 Hours," White House, March 17, 2003

[99] Colin Powell, "Secretary of State Colin L. Powell on ABC's *Oprah*," U.S. Department Of State: Office of the Spokesman, October 22, 2002, http://www.state.gov/secretary/rm/2002/14563.htm

[100] Condoleezza Rice, CNN's *Late Edition with Wolf Blitzer*, September 8, 2002

[101] George W. Bush, "President Bush Outlines Iraqi Threat; Remarks by the President on Iraq," Office of the Press Secretary, October 7, 2002, http://www.whitehouse.gov/news/releases/2002/10/20021007-8.html

[102] "The *Times* and Iraq," *New York Times*, May 26, 2004

[103] Brit Hume, FOX News Channel's *Special Report with Brit Hume*, July 6, 2004

[104] *The Harris Poll*, Harris Interactive, February 23, 2004

[105] http://mediamatters.org/static/special/poll-200405.pdf

[106] Timothy L. O'Brien, "U.N. Group Finds No Hussein-al Qaeda Link," *New York Times*, June 27, 2003

[107] Peter H. Stone, "Were Qaeda-Iraq Links Exaggerated?" *National Journal*, August 9, 2003

[108] The National Commission on Terrorist Attacks Upon the United States, "The 9/11 Commission Report," Chapter 2: The Foundation of the New Terrorism, p. 66, www.9-11commission.gov

[109] Sean Hannity, FOX News Channel's *Hannity and Colmes*, July 19, 2004

[110] Rush Limbaugh in a January 29, 2004 radio broadcast as reported in *The New American*. William F. Jasper, "No WMDs in Iraq? Why It Matters," *The New American*, February 23, 2004

[111] Ann Coulter, "Democrats Want Saddam Back; He Makes 'Em Look Moderate By Comparison," *Calgary Sun*, July 4, 2004

[112] Kelly Arena, CNN's *Wolf Blitzer Reports*, May 27, 2004

[113] Reuters, March 17, 2004

[114] *The Sean Hannity Show*, June 8, 2004

[115] Oliver North, FOX News Channel's *Hannity and Colmes*, February 12, 2002

[116] Oliver North, "Point Man for the Kosovo Come-On," *Washington Times*, February 8, 1999

[117] Mona Charen, "Continuing Saga. . . And a Question of Timing; Wag the Dog Attempt?" *Washington Times*, December 21, 1998

[118] Cal Thomas, "Congress shares the blame for intelligence failures," *Baltimore Sun*, July 14, 2004

[119] Department of Defense Casualty Report, *http://www.defenselink.mil/*, accessed August 9, 2004

[120] Ann Coulter, "Democrats Want Saddam Back; He Makes 'Em Look Moderate By Comparison," *Calgary Sun*, July 4, 2004

[121] Ann Coulter, "Democrats Want Saddam Back; He Makes 'Em Look Moderate By Comparison," *Calgary Sun*, July 4, 2004

[122] Ann Coulter, FOX News Channel's *The O'Reilly Factor*, May 27, 2004

[123] "Iraq Coalition Casualty Count," http://icasualties.org/oif/

[124] Joe Scarborough, MSNBC's *Scarborough Country*, May 17, 2004

[125] Putin Turns on US Over War in Iraq," Reuters, March 20, 2003

[126] "Vatican Slams US," The Australian, March 19, 2003

[127] Bill O'Reilly, *Who's Looking Out for You?*, New York: Broadway Books, 2003, p. 148

[128] Will Lester, "AP Poll: Abroad, Many Hold Negative View of Bush Role in World Affairs," *Associated Press*, March 4, 2004

[129] Will Lester, "AP Poll: Abroad, Many Hold Negative View of Bush Role in World Affairs,," *Associated Press*, March 4, 2004

[130] Charles Krauthammer, "A World Imagined," *The New Republic*, March 15, 1999

[131] Michael Hirsh, "Europe's Big Bet on a Bush 'Regime Change'," *Newsweek*, July 26, 2004

[132] Christopher Marquis, "Bush Faces New Obstacles In Keeping Allies' Support," *New York Times*, July 31, 2004

[133] Christopher Marquis, "Bush Faces New Obstacles In Keeping Allies' Support," *New York Times*, July 31, 2004

[134] Dana Milbank, "Opinion of U.S. Abroad Is Falling, Survey Finds," *Washington Post*, March 17, 2004

[135] Major Garret, FOX News Channel's *Special Report with Brit Hume*, March 17, 2004

[136] Oliver North, "Auditioning for Commander in Chief," *Washington Times*, August 27, 2000

[137] Dana Milbank, "Support for Troops Questioned," *Washington Post*, June 17, 2003

[138] Dana Milbank, "Support for Troops Questioned," *Washington Post*, June 17, 2003

[139] Edward Walsh, "Veterans Groups Critical of Bush's VA Budget," *Washington Post*, March 3, 2004

[140] William Douglas, "Bush Alienating Some Military Voters Who Helped Him Win in 2000," Knight Ridder Washington Bureau, March 14, 2004

[141] William Douglas, "Bush Alienating Some Military Voters Who Helped Him Win in 2000," Knight Ridder Washington Bureau, March 14, 2004

[142] Michael Savage, on MSNBC's *Scarborough Country*, May 2, 2003

[143] Rush Limbaugh, "The Largest Hypothalamus in North America," www.rushlimbaugh.com, January 6, 2003

[144] Rush Limbaugh, "Until You Pay for Health Care, Costs Won't Come Down," www.rushlimbaugh.com, November 20, 2003

[145] Hewitt Associates, Health Care Expectations: Future Strategy and Direction 2004

[146] "Rising Health care Costs Making Employers and Employees Sick," PricewaterhouseCoopers, April 1, 2004

[147] CDC, Health Insurance Coverage: Estimates from the National Health Interview Survey, 2003

[148] Employee Benefit Research Institute, Current Population Survey, March 1988-2003 Supplements

[149] "Re-Examining Medicare—The Drug Industry's Muscle," *New York Times*, September 5, 2003

[150] "Issue Advertising in the 1999-2000 Election Cycle," Issue Ads @ AAPC, A Project of the Annenberg Public Policy Center of the University of Pennsylvania

[151] Rush Limbaugh, "76 percent of Seniors Have Prescription Drug Coverage," www.rushlimbaugh.com, August 19, 2003

[152] Kaiser Family Foundation, "Medicare at a Glance," March 2004

[153] "Surfing for a Better Drug Deal," *New York Times*, June 6, 2004

[154] Families USA, "Low-Income Medicare Beneficiaries Are Most in Need of Prescription Drug Coverage," Fact Sheet

[155] Tucker Carlson, NBC's *The Chris Mathews Show*, November 30, 2003

[156] Families USA, "Medicare Proposal Denies Much-Needed Help 2.8 Million Lowest-Income Seniors," November 20, 2003

[157] Ann Coulter, "Stem-Cell Research Is Merely the Newest 'Cure-All' Craze," www.anncoulter.com, July 26, 2001

[158] Ann Coulter, "Stem-Cell Research Is Merely the Newest 'Cure-All' Craze," www.anncoulter.com, July 26, 2001

[159] University of Wisconsin press release, November 5, 1998 www.news.wisc.edu/packages/stemcells/3327.html

[160] University of Wisconsin Stem Cell Research Project, www.news.wisc.edu/packages/stemcells

[161] University of Wisconsin Stem Cell Research Project, www.news.wisc.edu/packages/stemcells

[162] American Association for the Advancement of Science, Stem Cell Research Policy Brief, www.aaas.org/spp/cstc/briefs/stemcells

[163] "Research caught in Election Impasse; Fate of Stem-Cell Lab on Hold, Official Says," Minneapolis Star Tribune, December 1, 2000

[164] Ann Coulter, "Let's Rewrite One for The Gipper!": Townhall.com, June 17 2004

[165] Union of Concerned Scientists, Scientific Integrity in Policy Making

[166] Rick Weiss, "Bush Ejects Two From Bioethics Council; Changes Renew Criticism That the President Puts Politics Ahead of Science," *Washington Post*, February 28, 2004

[167] Rush Limbaugh, "You Can't Make Everyone Like You," www.rushlimbaugh.com, January 29, 2004

[168] NORA Fiscal Year 2005 HIV/AIDS Appropriations Recommendations www.aidsaction.org/legislation/nora.htm

[169] NORA Fiscal Year 2002 HIV/AIDS Appropriations Recommendations www.aidsaction.org/legislation/nora.htm

[170] NORA Fiscal Year 2005 HIV/AIDS Appropriations Recommendations www.aidsaction.org/legislation/nora.htm

[171] National Institute of Allergy and Infectious Diseases, HIV/AIDS Statistics, July 2004

[172A] Rush Limbaugh, *The Rush Limbaugh Show*, June 9, 2004

[172B] Centers for Disease Control, http://www.cdc.gov/hiv/stats.htm#exposure

[172C] Department of Health and Human Services, http://www.niaid.nih.gov/factsheets/aidsstat.htm

[173] "Legal Malpractice: Will Congress side with the lawyers or the doctors?," *National Review*, March 24, 2003

[174] Bureau of Justice Statistics, 1996 www.ojp.usdoj.gov/bjs/abstract/cfjs96.htm

[175] National Practitioner Data Bank, Sept. 1, 1990–Sept. 30, 2002

[176] Kentucky Legislative Research Commission, The Costs of Medical Malpractice Insurance and its Effect on Health Care, Report, June 12, 2003

[177] Weiss Ratings, Inc., Medical Malpractice Caps: The Impact of Damage Caps on Physician Premiums, June 2, 2003

[178] "Limiting Tort Liability for Medical Malpractice," CBO, January 8, 2004

[179] Sean Hannity, Fox News Channel *Hannity and Colmes*, July 21, 2004

[180] American Insurance Association Press Release, March 13, 2002

[181] Abraham Lincoln's Last Public Address, Washington, D.C., April 11, 1865

[182] Rush Limbaugh, "We Spend More on Education Than Anything," September 18, 2003

[183] John Podhoretz, *Bush Country*, New York: St. Martin's Press, 2004

[184] H.Con.Res.76, House vote #345, May 18, 1995

[185] H.R.1158, House vote #251, March 16, 1995

[186] William Safire, "Vouchers Help Blacks," *New York Times*, August 21, 2000

[187] William Safire, "Vouchers Help Blacks," *New York Times*, August 21, 2000

[188] Michael Winerip, "What Some Much-Noted Data Really Showed About Vouchers" *New York Times*, May 7, 2003

[189] Brian P. Gill, P. Michael Timpane, Karen E. Ross, Dominic J. Brewer, "Rhetoric Versus Reality: What We Know and What We Need to Know About Vouchers and Charter Schools," Rand, 2001, http://www.rand.org/publications/MR/MR1118

[190] Nanette Asimov, "Vouchers Could Cost State Billions/Study warns of flaws in education measure," *San Francisco Chronicle*, September 20, 2000

[191] Fred Barnes, "Advantage Bush; They Would Have Preferred Dean, But the Bushies Are Still Confident," *The Weekly Standard*, February 2, 2004

[192] National Education Association, President's Budget Request For Fiscal Year 2005, Federal Education-Related Programs

[193] FOX News Channel's, *Hannity and Colmes*, January 28, 2000

[194] FOX News Channel's *Hannity and Colmes*, January 14, 2003

[195] U.S. Department of Commerce Economics and Statistics Administration, Bureau of the Census, "We the Americans: Our Education," September 1993

[196] U.S. Department of Commerce Economics and Statistics Administration, Bureau of the Census, "We the Americans: Our Education," September 1993

[197] Bill O'Reilly, *The O'Reilly Factor*, June 3, 2004

[198] Bill O'Reilly, *The Radio Factor with Bill O'Reilly*, July 7, 2004

[199] Bill O'Reilly, *The O'Reilly Factor*, July 21, 2004

[200] National Center for Education Statistics, *Digest of Education Statistics*, "Years of school 0 completed by persons age 25 and over and 25 to 29, by race/ethnicity and sex: 1910 to 2001"

[201] National Center for Education Statistics, *Digest of Education Statistics*, "College enrollment rates of high school completers, by race/ethnicity: 1960 to 2001"

[202] National Center for Education Statistics, *Digest of Education Statistics*, "Percent of public high school graduates taking selected mathematics and science courses in high school, by sex and race/ethnicity: 1982 to 2000"

[203] National Center for Education Statistics, *Digest of Education Statistics*, "Graduate enrollment in science and engineering programs in degree-granting institutions, by field of study: United States and outlying areas: 1988 to 2000"

[204] Rush Limbaugh, *The Rush Limbaugh Show*, April 7, 2004

[205] "The GOP's Guerilla War on Green Laws," *Business Week*, December 12, 1994

[206] Bill Lambrecht, "Republicans Swinging Ax at Regulators, Regulations, "*St. Louis Post-Dispatch*, February 5, 1995

[207] Union of Concerned Scientists, Restoring Scientific Integrity in Policy Making, February 18, 2004

[208] Union of Concerned Scientists, Restoring Scientific Integrity in Policy Making, February 18, 2004

[209] Ann Coulter, "Global Warming: The French Connection," May 28, 2003

[210] Bill O'Reilly, *The O'Reilly Factor*, January 15, 2004

[211] Ross Gelbspan, *The Heat is On: The High Stakes Battle Over Earth's Threatened* Climate, Addison-Wesley, 1997, p.11

[212] Pew Center on Global Climate Change, "Global Warming Basics," www.pewclimate.org/global-warming-basics/basic_science

[213] Gregory Crofton, "Climatologist: Global Warming could have consequences in Sierra" Tahoe Daily Tribune , July 8, 2004

[214] FOX News Channel's Sean Hannity, *Hannity and Colmes*, May 25, 2004

[215] CNN, "Experts cite 'strong evidence' of global warming,"January 13, 2000

[216] FOX News Channel's Sean Hannity, *Hannity and Colmes*, May 25, 2004

[217] James K. Glassman and Sallie L. Baliunas, "Bush Is Right on Global Warming . . . not that reporters would understand . . ." *The Weekly Standard*, June 25, 2001

[218] CNN, "Experts Cite 'Strong Evidence' of Global Warming," January 13, 2000

[219] Ross Gelbspan, *The Heat is On: The High Stakes Battle Over Earth's Threatened Climate*, Addison-Wesley, 1997, pp.57-58

[220] "U.S. Going Empty-Handed to Meeting on Global Warming," *New York Times*, March 29, 2001

[221] "2 Weeks Starting Today to Argue Fine and Crucial Details of Cutting Greenhouse Gas," *New York Times*, November 13, 2000

[222] FOX News Channel's Sean Hannity, *Hannity and Colmes*, June 27, 2003

[223] David Frum, "The Air War at Home," *National Review*, December 23, 2002

[224] FOX News Channel, *Hannity and Colmes*, August 3, 2004

[225] "Arsenic Gives Bush Record a Bitter Taste," *Newsday* editorial, April 22, 2001

[226] "White House Rejected a Stricter E.P.A. Alternative to the President's Clear Skies Plan," *New York Times*, April 28, 2002

[227] Natural Resources Defense Council, The Bush Administration's Air Pollution Plan, www.nrdc.org/air/pollution/fclearsk.asp

[228] "Cloudy Skies," *New York Times* editorial, April 28, 2002

[229] Ann Coulter, "It's a Wonder Republicans Ever Win," *National Post*, December 12, 2003

[230] Steven Moore as interviewed in "RINO Hunter; The Club for Growth Had a Great Election Day," The American Spectator, November 2002-December 2002

[231] Lydia Saad, "Retirement Planning Leads Americans' Financial Worry List," The Gallup Organization Poll Analysis, May 18, 2004

[232] Christine Dugas, "American Seniors Rack Up Debt Like Never Before," *USA Today*, April 25, 2002

[233] Christine Dugas, "American Seniors Rack Up Debt Like Never Before," *USA Today*, April 25, 2002

[234] Sean Hannity, *Let Freedom Ring, Winning the War of Liberty Over Liberalism*, New York: HarperCollins Publishers Inc., 2002, p. 243

[235] George W. Bush, "Renewing America's Purpose," Speech in Rancho Cucamonga, May 15, 2000

[236] George W. Bush, Speech to Republican National Convention, August 3, 2000

[237] Jonathan Weisman and Richard Benedetto, "Bush Backs off Pledge for Social Security," *USA Today*, August 28, 2001

[238] Sean Hannity, FOX News Channel's *Hannity and Colmes*, August 14, 2002

[239] Christine Hall, "Democrats Conspire to 'Scare Seniors' About Social Security," CNSNews.com, May 24, 2002

[240] The Bulletin's Frontrunner, September 4, 2001

[241] Former Republican Senate Whip Alan Simpson of Wyoming as Quoted in "The AARP and the GOP," CNN.com, November 24, 2003

[242] National Committee to Preserve Social Security and Medicare Department of Policy Research, "Social Security,", May 24, 2004

[243] National Committee to Preserve Social Security and Medicare Department of Policy Research, "Myths and Realities about the Future of Social Security," April 22, 2004

[244] Center for Responsive Politics, "2004 Presidential Race," www.opensecrets.com

[245] David Limbaugh, "Democrats Demagogue Social Security," Townhall.com, July 28, 2001

[246] National Committee to Preserve Social Security and Medicare, Department of Policy Research, "Social Security," May 24, 2004

[247] National Committee to Preserve Social Security and Medicare, Department of Policy Research, "Myths and Realities about the Future of Social Security," April 22, 2004

[248] National Committee to Preserve Social Security and Medicare, Department of Policy Research, "Social Security," May 24, 2004

[249] Richard W. Stevenson, "Bush Panel Outlines 3 Plans for Social Security Overhaul," *New York Times*, November 30, 2001

[250] *The Rush Limbaugh Show*, July 26, 1995

[251] *The Rush Limbaugh Show*, July 26, 1995

[252] *The Rush Limbaugh Show*, July 26, 1995

[253] Newt Gingrich, Speech to Blue Cross Blue Shield, October 2, 1995

[254] Linda Chavez, CNN's *Capital Gang Sunday*, September 24, 1995

[255] Robert Pear and Robin Toner, "Bush Drug Proposal in Medicare Plan Faces Stiff Battle," *New York Times*, May 21, 2003

[256] *Congressional Record*, March 19, 2003

[257] Robert Pear and Robin Toner, "President Leads the Roundup for Votes to Add Drug Benefits to Medicare," *New York Times*, June 26, 2003

[258] Robert Pear and Robin Toner, "Bush Drug Proposal in Medicare Plan Faces Stiff Battle," *New York Times*, May 21, 2003

[259] Charles Krauthammer, FOX News Channel's *On the Record with Greta Van Susteren*, January 29, 2003

[260] Charles Krauthammer, "Best Use for the Tax Surplus Is to Retire Debt with It," Desert News August 1, 1999

[261] Tucker Carlson, NBC's *The Chris Mathews Show*, November 30, 2003

[262] Christine Dugas, "American Seniors Rack Up Debt Like Never Before," *USA Today*, April 25, 2002

[263] Christine Dugas, "American Seniors Rack Up Debt Like Never Before," *USA Today*, April 25, 2002

[264] Laura Ingraham, MSNBC's *Hardball*, December 19, 2003

[265] Kellyanne Conway, FOX News Channel's *Hannity and Colmes*, March 1, 2004

[266] Fred Barnes, FOX News Channel's *The Beltway Boys*, November 29, 2003

[267] National Committee to Preserve Social Security and Medicare, Government Relations and Policy/Policy Research, "Viewpoint: The New Medicare Law: A Bad Deal for Seniors," May 25, 2004

[268] National Committee to Preserve Social Security and Medicare, Press Release, "Medicare Drug Card: Delivering Savings for Participating Beneficiaries," June 8, 2004

[269] Shweta Govindarajan, "House GOP Returns Fire on Drug Cards: Thomas Says Dem Criticism Seeks to Distort Plan," *The Hill*, May 13, 2004

[270] AFL-CIO, "Seniors Board the Rx Express to Buy Affordable Medication in Canada," July 20, 2004 <http://www.aflcio.org/issuespolitics/medicare/ns07202004.cfm>

[271] Senator Jay Rockefeller, FOX News Channel's *Special Report with Brit Hume,* January 30, 2004

[272] FOX News Channel's, *The O'Reilly Factor*, December 23, 2003

[273] Eric Lichtblau, "For Voters, Osama Replaces the Common Criminal," *New York Times*, July 18, 2004

[274] Eric Lichtblau, "For Voters, Osama Replaces the Common Criminal," *New York Times*, July 18, 2004

[275] Kevin Johnson, "Mean Streets Once Again: Gang Activity Surging," *USA Today*, July 21, 2004

[276] Kevin Johnson, "Mean Streets Once Again: Gang Activity Surging," *USA Today*, July 21, 2004

[277] International Brotherhood of Police Officers press release, May 14, 2004

[278] Eric Lichtblau, "For Voters, Osama Replaces the Common Criminal," *New York Times*, July 18, 2004

[279] Alison Mitchell, "Bush Says the Clinton Administration Waged a Lackluster War on Illegal Drugs," *New York Times*, October 7, 2000

[280] Clay Johnson, "Testimony," Office of Management and Budget, May 6, 2004 http://www.whitehouse.gov/omb/legislative/testimony/cjohnson/040506_cjohnson_attach.pdf

[281] Eric Lichtblau, "For Voters, Osama Replaces the Common Criminal," *New York Times*, July 18, 2004

[282] Thomas Sowell, "GOP Will Recover, Nation May Not," *Rocky Mountain News*, July 3, 1996

[283] Thomas Sowell, "GOP Will Recover, Nation May Not," *Rocky Mountain News*, July 3, 1996

[284] Richard Lessner, "On Safari. Christmas in July, Inventing Rights," *Union Leader*, July 15, 1996

[285] "Clinton's odd brand of justice," *Tampa Tribune*, February 2, 1996

[286] Cal Thomas, "The Two Visions," *Times-Picayune*, January 27, 1996

[287] "Crime Drops Across U.S. Experts Warn of Next Wave," *Denver Post*, May 6, 1996

[288] "Crime drops across U.S. Experts Warn of Next Wave," *Denver Post*, May 6, 1996

[289] "Crime drops across U.S. Experts Warn of Next Wave," *Denver Post*, May 6, 1996

[290] "Crime drops across U.S. Experts Warn of Next Wave," *Denver Post*, May 6, 1996

[291] Mona Charen, "About Those COPS," Townhall.com, May 13, 2003

[292] Rowan Scarborough, "Ensuring Reagan's place in history," *Washington Times*, February 1, 1998

[293] Editorial, "Gun Control, Ashcroft Style," *Wall Street Journal*, February 3, 2003

[294] Mark Murray, "Issues of the Day, Where Bush Stands," *National Journal*, August 7, 1999

[295] John Ashcroft, "Transcript," National Community Policing Conference, July 15, 2002

[296] John Ashcroft, "Transcript," National Community Policing Conference, July 15, 2002

[297] Curt Anderson, "Bush Budget Questions COPS Program," Associated Press Online, February 3, 2003

[298] Robert Pear, "Opposition Builds To Spending Cuts In Bush's Budget," *New York Times*, April 9, 2001

[299] Curt Anderson, "Bush Budget Questions COPS Program," Associated Press Online, February 3, 2003

[300] Press Release, "'Flawed Budget' for 2005 Would Fail to Keep Communities Strong," National League of Cities, February 3, 2004

[301] Editorial, "Whose Drug Problem," *Wall Street Journal*, August 28, 1997

[302] Alison Mitchell, "Bush Says the Clinton Administration Waged a Lackluster War on Illegal Drugs," *New York Times*, October 7, 2000

[303] Alison Mitchell, "Bush Says the Clinton Administration Waged a Lackluster War on Illegal Drugs," *New York Times*, October 7, 2000

[304] Clay Johnson, "Testimony," Office of Management and Budget, May 6, 2004 http://www.whitehouse.gov/omb/legislative/testimony/cjohnson/040506_cjohnson_attach.pdf

[305] George W. Bush, "President Proclaims National Domestic Violence Awareness Month," Office of the Press Secretary, October 2, 2001

[306] George W. Bush "National Domestic Violence Awareness Month, 2003," Office of the Press Secretary, October 8, 2003

[307] Patty Murray, "Remarks by Senator Patty Murray Introducing the Paul & Sheila Wellstone Domestic Violence Prevention Amendment,"States News Service, March 25, 2004

[308] Ann Coulter, "To Mock a Mockingbird" *Jewish World Review* February 8, 2000

[309] James Alan Fox, "Washington Cuts Bucks for Badges; Bush Administration Adds Terrorist Fight to the burdens of Local Police Departments, Then Slices Funding," *Newsday*, April 21, 2004

[310] Robert Pear, "White House Trumpets Programs It Tried to Cut," *New York Times*, May 19, 2004

[311] James Alan Fox, "Washington Cuts Bucks For Badges; Bush Administration Adds Terrorist Fight to the Burdens of Local Police Departments, Then Slices Funding," *Newsday*, April 21, 2004

[312] Eric Lichtblau, "For Voters, Osama Replaces the Common Criminal," *New York Times*, July 18, 2004

[313] Eric Lichtblau, "For Voters, Osama Replaces the Common Criminal," *New York Times*, July 18, 2004

[314] James Alan Fox, "Washington Cuts Bucks For Badges; Bush Administration Adds Terrorist Fight to the Burdens of Local Police Departments, Then Slices Funding," *Newsday*, April 21, 2004

[315] James Alan Fox, "Washington Cuts Bucks For Badges; Bush Administration Adds Terrorist Fight to the Burdens of Local Police Departments, Then Slices Funding," *Newsday*, April 21, 2004;

[316] Fox Butterfield, "As Cities Struggle, Police Get By With Less," *New York Times*, July 27, 2004

[317] Mona Charen, "We Have to Win," September 9, 2003

[318] Sarah Kershaw, "Governors Tell of War's Impact on Local Needs," *New York Times*, July 20, 2004

[319] Sarah Kershaw, "Governors Tell of War's Impact on Local Needs," *New York Times*, July 20, 2004

[320] Sarah Kershaw, "Governors Tell of War's Impact on Local Needs," *New York Times*, July 20, 2004

[321] Sarah Kershaw, "Governors Tell of War's Impact on Local Needs," *New York Times*, July 20, 2004

[322] Sarah Kershaw, "Governors Tell of War's Impact on Local Needs," *New York Times*, July 20, 2004

[323] Sarah Kershaw, "Governors Tell of War's Impact on Local Needs," *New York Times*, July 20, 2004

[324] Sarah Kershaw, "Governors Tell of War's Impact on Local Needs," *New York Times*, July 20, 2004

[325] Sean Hannity, *Let Freedom Ring: Winning the War of Liberty Over Liberalism*, New York: HarperCollins Publishers Inc., 2002, p. 108

[326] Sean Hannity, *Let Freedom Ring: Winning the War of Liberty Over Liberalism*, New York: HarperCollins Publishers Inc., 2002, p. 108

[327] Eric Lichtblau, "For Voters, Osama Replaces the Common Criminal," *New York Times*, July 18, 2004

[328] Patrick Buchanan, Nominating Speech at the Republican National Convention, August 17, 1992

[329] James Taranto, "Best of the Web Today," OpinionJournal.com, May 17, 2004

[330] Thomas Frank, *What's the Matter with Kansas: How Conservatives Won the Heart of America*, Metropolitan 2004, p. 6

[331] James Taranto, "Best of the Web Today," OpinionJournal.com, June 16, 2004

[332] FOX News Channel's, *Special Report*, July 26, 2004

[333] FOX News Channel's, *The Big Story with John Gibson*, July 26, 2004

[334] Ann Coulter, "The Democrats Are all the Same," *National Post* (Canada), January 23, 2004

[335] Federal Census Bureau, Vital Statistics of The Day, www.census.gov/prod/2004pubs/03statab/vitstat.pdf

[336] Michael Savage, *The Enemy Within: Saving America from the Liberal Assault on Our Schools, Faith, and Military*, WND Books, 2004, p. 182

[337] Centers for Disease Control, National Center for Health Care Statistics, www.cdc.gov/nchs/data/hus/tables/2003/03hus017.pdf

[338] Centers for Disease Control, National Center for Health Care Statistics, www.cdc.gov/nchs/data/hus/tables/2003/03hus017.pdf

[339] Sean Hannity, *Let Freedom Ring,* New York: HarperCollins Publishers Inc., 2002, p. 286

[340] Chris Wallace, *FOX News Convention Coverage,* July 27, 2004

[341] Federal Census Bureau, *Vital Statistics of The Day,* www.census.gov/prod/2004pubs/03statab/vitstat.pdf

[342] FOX News Channel's, *Hannity and Colmes,* October 26, 2001

[343] John Kerry, Democratic National Convention Acceptance speech, July 29, 2004, www.johnkerry.com/pressroom/speeches/spc_2004_0729.html

[344] Rep. Rom DeLay (R-TX), *Congressional Record,* September 10, 1992

[345] Michael Wines, "Bush Vetoes Bill Making Employers Give Family Leave," *New York Times,* September 23, 1992

[346] Opinion Page Editorial, "Family-Leave Time Is Good Business," *Business Week,* September 28, 1992

[347] Todd S. Purdum, "Clinton Talks of Welfare and Family Leave," *New York Times,* September 11, 1996

[348] Debra Nussbaum, "Hitting a Bump in the Medical Leave Law," January 18, 1998

[349] Michael Savage, *Savage Nation,* August 3, 2004

[350] Steve Rothaus, "Being Gay Has Nothing to do with Pedophilia," the *Miami Herald,* January 15, 2002

[351] Paul Morton, International Presiding Bishop of the Full Gospel Fellowship and Pastor of the Greater St. Stephen Missionary Baptist Church, MSNBC'S *Scarborough Country,* May 17, 2004

[352] Nathaniel Frank, "Perverted," *The New Republic,* May 3, 2004, p. 20

[353] Nathaniel Frank, "Perverted," *The New Republic,* May 3, 2004, p. 20

[354] Michael Savage, *Savage Nation* (Radio), July 28, 2004

[355] Steve Rendall, "An Aggressive Conservative vs. a 'Liberal to be Determined': The false balance of *Hannity and Colmes,*" *Extra!* November/December 2003, www.fair.org

Media Matters Action Network is the advocacy organization associated with *Media Matters for America,* a new not-for-profit web-based research and information center in Washington, D.C. that monitors, analyzes, and corrects conservative misinformation in the U.S. media. In just a few short months, *Media Matters for America,* founded by David Brock, author of *Blinded by the Right: The Conscience of an Ex-Conservative* and *The Republican Noise Machine: Right-Wing Media and How It Corrupts Democracy,* has established itself as a key resource on conservative misinformation for both producers and consumers of news. In its first three months, mediamatters.org has served more than one million visitors. Visit mediamatters.org and get involved in holding the news media accountable.

Akashic Books is a New York City–based independent company dedicated to publishing urban literary fiction and political nonfiction by authors who are either ignored by the mainstream, or who have no interest in working within the ever-consolidating ranks of the major corporate publishers. Akashic Books hosts additional imprints, including RDV Books, Punk Planet Books, the Akashic U.S. Presidents Series, and Dennis Cooper's "Little House on the Bowery" fiction series.

For more information, visit www.akashicbooks.com, email Akashic7@aol.com, or write us at Akashic Books, PO Box 1456, New York, NY, 10009.